After Removal
The Choctaw in Mississippi

After Removal

The Choctaw in Mississippi

Edited by
Samuel J. Wells
and
Roseanna Tubby

UNIVERSITY PRESS OF MISSISSIPPI
Jackson and London

Copyright © 1986 by the
University Press of Mississippi and Choctaw Heritage Press

All rights reserved

Manufactured in the United States of America

Print-On-Demand Edition

This book has been sponsored by the Choctaw Heritage Press, Philadelphia, Mississippi, and has been partially funded by the U.S. Department of Education, Office of Indian Programs. The opinions expressed herein do not necessarily represent the views of the Mississippi Band of Choctaw Indians, nor do they represent the views of the United States Department of Education, Indian Education Program, Title IV, Part B.

Library of Congress Cataloging-in-Publication Data Available

ISBN 1-57806-684-0

Contents

Introduction   vii

1   The Mississippi Choctaw: From the Removal Treaty to the Federal Agency   *Ronald N. Satz*   3

2   Choctaw Farmsteads in Mississippi, 1830   *Rufus Ward*   33

3   The Role of Mixed-Bloods in Mississippi Choctaw History   *Samuel J. Wells*   42

4   Chief Greenwood Leflore and His Malmaison Plantation   *R. Halliburton, Jr.*   56

5   The Choctaw Struggle for Land and Identity in Mississippi, 1830–1918   *Clara Sue Kidwell*   64

6   The Second Choctaw Removal, 1903   *Charles Roberts*   94

7   Holy Rosary Indian Mission: The Mississippi Choctaw and the Catholic Church   *Sister John Christopher Langford, M.S.B.T.*   112

8   Economic Progress and Development in the Mississippi Band of Choctaw Indians since 1945   *Jesse O. McKee and Steve Murray*   122

Selected Bibliography   137

Contributors   147

Index   149

Tribal Credits

Tribal Chief
Phillip Martin

Director,
Choctaw Department of Eudcation
Robert J. Swan

Director,
Research and Curriculum Development
William Brescia

Tribal Publication Review Committee
Beasley Denson
Robert B. Ferguson
Thomas L. Goldman
Thallis Lewis

The opinions expressed herein do not necessarily represent the view of the Mississippi Band of Choctaw Indians, nor do they represent the view of the United States Department of Education, Indian Education program, Title IV, part B.

Introduction

After the signing of the Treaty of Dancing Rabbit Creek in 1830, the U.S. government began the methodical removal of the Choctaw Indians from their native land in present-day Mississippi, uprooting about 20,000 of the estimated 25,000 tribesmen in the process. What became of the thousands of people who remained? A few hundred households stayed behind with government approval and were given individual parcels of land reservations as a treaty stipulation. Some other Choctaw—mixed-bloods who had already abandoned their ancestral ways and had chosen white culture as a life-style—simply merged with the incoming white settlers and stayed in the community as white people. Several thousand Indians, however, faded into the wilderness until they were forced out by an expanding white population.

This book tells the story of the third group of people. The subject of the Indian removal has already been examined at length by several renowned historians, but the more poignant saga of the many Choctaw who escaped removal has received suprisingly scant attention. Aside from the probing dissertation that John H. Peterson, Jr., wrote in 1970 and the occasional article that has been published in the regional journals, the topic has remained largely uninvestigated.

Research by both local observers and nationally recognized scholars was sought so that this anthology could explore the widest range of experiences of the Mississippi Choctaw. By means of this volume and others, the Mississippi Band of Choctaw Indians seeks better understanding of the Choctaw through a thorough examination of their past. The latest research by historians, geographers, anthropologists, educators, and community researchers interested in the Mississippi Choctaw, assembled here, spans several disciplines and perspectives. The slight overlap in time periods and topics and the lacuna—no chapter deals with the years 1918–1945—is more a bonus than a problem, for it suggests the abundance of research materials and readily indicates where more work is needed.

The eight authors who have contributed chapters to the book have

Introduction

varied backgrounds. Most hail from the academic community. Several have published earlier works on the Choctaw Indians. Several others are primarily community researchers whose close contact and work with the Mississippi Choctaw have given them a unique perspective.

In discussing the period 1830–1918, Ronald Satz gives us a broad foundation from which to study the postremoval sufferings of the Mississippi Choctaw. His survey of Jacksonian Indian policy, of the land fraud inflicted upon many Mississippi Choctaw, and of later efforts to arrange for the Mississippi group's acceptance as wards of the federal government offers a thorough overview of Mississippi Choctaw history prior to their eventual recognition by the federal government.

"Choctaw Farmsteads in Mississippi, 1830" by Rufus Ward, a practicing attorney, addresses the question of settlement patterns and the life-style of removal-era Mississippi Choctaw. Rather than attempt to describe the entire Choctaw Nation, Ward studies three counties in the northeastern Choctaw district, examining the many land and legal records of the area in order to depict early nineteenth-century Choctaw life. Since this area soon developed into prime cotton land, Ward's research increases our understanding of conditions along a cultural frontier where white land speculators competed directly with the Indians for control of the arable acreage.

In the same investigative spirit, I have written about a crucial portion of the Indian population, the often overlooked Choctaw mixed-bloods. Using largely untapped land records and Indian genealogical sources I examine both the origins and the nature of the mixed-bloods and ask whether the study of Indian-white relations has too often focused on the extremes of differences between Indians and whites and not enough on the similarities of their cultures as dynamically integrated in the mixed-blood. To what degree did the mixed bloods control and influence the Choctaw councils prior to removal? How large a group were they? Who were they? I endeavor to answer these questions, and others, in the process naming many of these bicultural pioneers and analyzing the actions of the most prominent individuals.

R. Halliburton, Jr. discusses the life of the legendary Greenwood Leflore, one of the most prominent mixed bloods. Tracing Leflore's French-Canadian roots, Halliburton also examines his controversial role in negotiating the removal treaty at Dancing Rabbit Creek and his

Introduction

rise to affluence as a plantation owner and state senator. Leflore's success is amply attested by his opulent plantation, Malmaison, which memorialized the mixed-blood's financial achievements until it burned to the ground in 1942. Although a few other Choctaw mixed-bloods who remained in Mississippi also achieved financial success and cultural acceptance, none accumulated wealth that could rival Leflore's.

At the bottom of the economic ladder were several thousand Choctaw, mostly full-bloods, who pursued their traditional ways until the disappearance of game and arable land forced them into quasi-slavery doing odd jobs or sharecropping. Unable to wrest a living from nature, these impoverished Indians sought work among white farmers as cotton pickers and unskilled laborers. Not until late in the nineteenth century was a major effort undertaken to assist them, an effort that centered near the Choctaw population concentrations in Neshoba County, Mississippi.

Leading one effort to aid the Choctaw, the Catholic church under Bishop Francis Janssens, then bishop of Natchez, opened Holy Rosary Indian Mission early in the 1880s. The attempts by religious workers to obtain farmland and to found schools for the Indians are traced by Sister John Christopher, whose knowledge of reservation life and the Catholic missionary presence among the Choctaw give her a unique perspective. Her analysis illuminates the Mississippi Choctaw struggle from the founding of the mission until the "second removal" at the turn of the twentieth century.

The partially successful effort to remove the remaining Mississippi Choctaw to Oklahoma stemmed from the Dawes commission's efforts to indentify nonreservation Indians and place them in Indian Territory, where, it was thought, existing programs could better address their needs. Some of the survivors whose ancestors had eluded the first removal now acquiesced to federal and local demands and made the journey westward across the Mississippi River where the old Indian Territory was evolving into the state of Oklahoma. A tenacious few still refused to leave their ancestral homelands, however, and today form the nucleus of the Mississippi Band of Choctaw Indians.

Clara Sue Kidwell discusses the period between the 1830 removal and the emergence of the Mississippi Band of Choctaw Indians, with

Introduction

an emphasis on land allotments and schools. Kidwell draws heavily upon the federal legislative records to determine the role that land speculation played in the postremoval Choctaw saga. She also analyzes the writings of educator and historian Henry Sales Halbert to understand the condition of the Mississippi Choctaw during this time. Her chapter traces their plight into the second decade of the twentieth century.

Charles Roberts addresses in greater detail the government's effort to identify and remove the Mississippi Choctaw a second time at the turn of the century. He examines the events preceding the second removal, also briefly considering the labors of several religious missionary groups and some Oklahoma Choctaw to bring some of their Mississippi kinsmen west to Indian Territory. In addition he discusses the role of the Dawes commission hearings in Mississippi in identifying the Choctaw survivors and traces the fate of individuals who were later removed to the West.

Jesse McKee and Steve Murray pick up the thread of the Choctaw story after the Indians were officially embraced by the federal government, during and after World War II. McKee and Murray concentrate on the economic and political growth of the Mississippi Band as it grew to assume greater control over its own welfare and destiny. Their survey of the growing Choctaw industrial base and the Indians' search for greater self-reliance completes the book and brings the reader into the modern period.

William Brescia, director, Research and Curriculum Development, Mississippi Band of Choctaw Indians, greatly contributed to the concept and content of this volume, and the editors thank him for his assistance. They also extend special thanks to Neal Starkman, Charles Henley, Patricia Galloway and Carolyn Reeves; they are grateful to Agnes King, Marian V. Issac, and Esterline Isaac for their help in typing. Roseanna Tubby especially acknowledges the support of Father Robert J. Goodyear, whose unfailing encouragement helped her understand the advantage of being Choctaw.

Samuel J. Wells

After Removal
The Choctaw in Mississippi

1

The Mississippi Choctaw: From the Removal Treaty to the Federal Agency

Ronald N. Satz

Several generations of scholars have investigated the treatment of the southern Indian tribes during the Jacksonian era. Since Andrew Jackson was one of those rare individuals who left his imprint on an era, and since his Indian policy was quite controversial, the considerable attention granted him by historians is readily understandable, especially in connection with the so-called Trail of Tears.[1] Until recently, however, the postremoval experiences of Indian groups who continued to reside in the South after the removal era of the 1830s have been largely neglected by scholars.[2] The Indians who refused to heed President Jackson's removal policy included several thousand members of the Choctaw Nation, the first tribe to sign a treaty under the Removal Act of 1830. The experiences of these Choctaw and their descendants between 1833 and 1918 illuminate the legacy of Jackson's Indian removal policy.[3]

In mid-September 1830, barely four months after Jackson had pushed the Indian Removal Act through Congress, Secretary of War John Eaton arrived in Mississippi to persuade the Choctaw to sign a removal treaty under the new law. It was no accident that the Jackson administration focused its attention on the Choctaw. The Indians who

---

An earlier version of this chapter was presented at the forty-eighth annual meeting of the Southern Historical Association in Memphis, Tennessee, on November 4, 1982. I am grateful to the National Endowment for the Humanities for its support of my research, to my colleagues at the University of Tennessee at Martin and the University of Wisconsin–Eau Claire for their encouragement, and to W. Stitt Robinson, Arrell M. Gibson, and W. David Baird for their thoughtful comments on an early draft.

The site on Dancing Rabbit Creek where the treaty was signed in 1830.
Photo: Mary Ann Wells

assembled at Dancing Rabbit Creek in present-day Noxubee County to meet Eaton belonged to a powerful southern tribe second in size only to the Cherokee. The Choctaw had played a significant role in the diplomacy of the lower Mississippi Valley for generations. Jackson had long considered them a tremendous obstruction to American development in the strategic Southwest. Choctaw claims in central and southern Mississippi severely limited white landholding. Hoping to tighten America's grip in the lower Mississippi Valley by securing a removal treaty that would have "a controlling effect" on other southern tribes, the secretary of war used threats and bribes to persuade various

From the Removal Treaty Onward

Choctaw leaders to sign the land cession treaty on September 27 and 28.[4]

By the time of Eaton's parley with the Choctaw in Mississippi, opposition to the Indian Removal Act had become an important moral and political issue. A well-organized campaign by anti-Jackson politicians sought the support of influential religious spokesmen to help arouse the moral indignation of the American people against the president's Indian policy. Especially under attack was Jackson's contention that the extension of state laws over the southern tribes left the federal government powerless to protect the Indians unless they emigrated to the West. Some Americans feared that Jackson intended to force the southern tribes to leave, even though the Removal Act specified that emigration was to be voluntary.[5] Aware of this situation, Secretary of War Eaton, who personally handled the negotiations in Mississippi, inserted several provisions in the final document not only to woo influential tribal leaders into signing away their tribal land but also to convince U.S. senators (who would be asked to ratify the treaty) and their colleagues in the House of Representatives (who would be asked to appropriate funds to execute it) that the document had not been forced upon the Choctaw and that it served the best interests of the "beleaguered Indians" (in the phrase of some religious spokesmen and many anti-Jacksonites) as well as those of the United States.[6]

Three of the most important concessions concerned land allotments. Many "special reservations" ranging in size from 320 acres to 2,560 acres were awarded to various men whose services, needs, or influence, in the view of government representatives, simply had to be recognized. In addition to these bribes, Eaton agreed to offer two other kinds of land allotments in order to secure the treaty. Families that had cultivated the soil and had made improvement on their lands were promised 80–320 acres of land that they could sell, depending on the quantity of land that they had actually farmed, in order to pay their debts and to help finance their resettlement and new activities in the West. Finally, to quiet the vocal opposition of the vast majority of the tribe, Eaton promised in Article 14 that an unlimited number of allotments would be available to Choctaw families who wanted to remain in Mississippi and to become citizens of the state. Each Choctaw head of family could qualify for 640 acres of land and would be eligible to receive an additional 320 acres for every unmarried child over the age of ten with another 160 acres for each child under ten. After living on the land for five years, the Indian homesteaders would receive title in fee simple and would become citizens. Only these three concessions, and most especially Article 14, enabled Eaton to secure the signatures necessary to conclude the Treaty of Dancing Rabbit Creek.[7]

In negotiating the Choctaw treaty, Eaton assumed that only so-called civilized Indians, highly acculturated mixed-bloods with extensive property holdings, including black slaves, would actually remain in Mississippi under the provisions of Article 14. Eaton hoped that, except for perhaps 200 or so mixed bloods, the entire tribe, numbering more than 20,000 people, would emigrate.[8] To help ensure that the full-bloods, who constituted the overwhelming majority of the tribe, would not seek to invoke Article 14, Eaton repeatedly warned them of the many hardships that would befall them if they attempted to live under the laws of Mississippi. In other words, Article 14 was designed to illustrate the "liberal" policy of the federal government while guaranteeing to the satisfaction of the secretary of war that the Jackson administration would not actually need to demonstrate its liberality in the case of any great number of Indians. Eaton, however, had badly miscalculated. Despite the treaty's acceptance by some leaders, most full-bloods showed little interest in abandoning their homes or the sacred places in their tribal estate.[9]

The Treaty of Dancing Rabbit Creek, like other Indian land cession treaties in American history, was a device by which federal officials conveniently converted communally owned tribal lands into public domain open to sale, ostensibly for the benefit of land-hungry settlers but all too often for the benefit of greedy speculators. Although the Removal Act specified that the Indians should be fairly compensated for ceded lands, the remuneration provided by the government frequently left much to be desired from the Native American perspective. For most Choctaw, like other southern Indians, land had a meaning and value that could not be adequately measured in monetary terms.[10] Furthermore, as historian Dorothy V. Jones recently observed in *License for Empire: Colonialism by Treaty in Early America*, "in return for their land, the American Indians received goods, which were quickly consumed; money, which was soon spent; and certain rights and privileges, which few Indians had the knowledge or power to use effectively at the time the rights were granted." In later years, however, treaty rights frequently became the focus of legal battles between various states and Indian groups that had become both knowledgeable about and determined to defend the rights their ancestors had been able to obtain from federal negotiators.[11] Such has been the case of the Mississippi Choctaw with regard to Article 14 of the Treaty of Dancing Rabbit Creek.

The immediate effect of the signing of the Treaty of Dancing Rabbit Creek was the outbreak of intratribal conflict. Opposition to the treaty, especially its provisions for a land cession and for removal operations, became an issue in the factional strife between highly acculturated mixed-bloods, who typically accepted removal as inevitable, and the full-bloods, who were generally steadfast in their opposition to it. Eaton and other administration officials publicly blamed opposition to the treaty, including threats against the lives of the tribal leaders who signed it, on the activities of misguided individuals who exploited the "ignorance" of the full-bloods. Meanwhile, Eaton used several strategies to bind the Choctaw to the removal provision of the treaty, which specified that groups of emigrants should leave in the fall of 1831 and in the fall of each of the two following years. He threatened the dissidents with imprisonment and dispatched a cavalry company to maintain "law and order" and thereby to assure the tribe's fulfillment of the treaty provisions. Finally, Eaton directly interfered in the tribal internal affairs by refusing to recognize any chiefs other than those who had signed the treaty. Such actions persuaded some 15,000 Choctaw to leave Mississippi.[12]

About 6,000 Choctaw, 300 times the number Eaton had predicted, remained in Mississippi when the War Department terminated its removal operations at the end of 1833.[13] Under Article 14, Indians who wished to stay had six months following the treaty's ratification during which they could register with Agent William Ward for their land allotments. Inasmuch as the Senate had ratified the treaty and President Jackson had signed it into law in February 1831, the Choctaw could register until late August of that year. Eaton's treaty had failed to specify the exact procedures to be used in registering Article 14 claimants, so officicals in the War Department told Agent Ward to act on his own initiative and judgment. During the early nineteenth century, when America was a nation of loosely connected communities, the implementation of Indian treaties and federal laws frequently depended heavily on the intelligence, character, integrity, and interests of scattered field officials such as Ward. Some Indian field service agents cared little about Indian treaty rights. Such was certainly the case with Ward, who, astonished by the large numbers of Choctaw seeking to register under Article 14, repeatedly turned most of them away, even those who had traveled great distances from their villages to seek him out.[14]

Some full-bloods who spoke little if any English probably did not understand the specific procedures or requirements for registering. Even those who did, however, found themselves without effective power to protect their rights. Nevertheless, they refused to abandon their homeland. The majority of the 4,000 Choctaw living in Mississippi today have direct kinship ties to Indians who resisted removal in the 1830s.

The Choctaw who remained in Mississippi after 1833 were victims of one of the most flagrant cases of fraud, intimidation, and speculation in American history. Although the Senate took six months to ratify the treaty, squatters and speculators began moving in immediately after the negotiations. As whites inundated the Choctaw cession, the War Department made some efforts to evict the intruders in accordance with the terms of the treaty. The influx of Americans continued, however, and the actions of Agent Ward not only encouraged white squatters and speculators but also blatantly obstructed the treaty rights of the Choctaw.[15]

Increasing political pressure caused the Jackson administration to question the expediency of removing white intruders from the Choctaw cession. Agent Ward's assurances that there was really no conflict between the Indians and the whites were relayed by the War Department to President Jackson, who announced his great pleasure in learning that the presence of the Americans was totally "acceptable and useful" to the Choctaw and that he would not have to execute the provision of the treaty calling for the removal of the intruders.[16]

Abandoned by their federal agent, Article 14 claimants turned to local law enforcement officials for assistance. Although the state of Mississippi had actually extended its legal jurisdiction over the Indians before the treaty was negotiated, local officials frequently allied themselves with either squatters or speculators and were unconcerned about the rights of Indians. U.S. Marshall Anthony Campbell was an eyewitness to the harassment of the Choctaw by local officials, but Campbell maintained that he was helpless to assist the Indians. "The Choctaw Indians are, in all civil relations, viewed as citizens of the State" he advised the War Department. As a good Jacksonian Democrat, Campbell also informed his superiors that he hesitated to take action against "respectable and intelligent" white intruders, fearing that such actions would be "very objectionable, as a measure of the administration, to a considerable portion of the people of Tennessee, Alabama, Louisiana, and Mississippi." State courts offered the Indians a vehicle for seeking redress, but the legal process was costly, time consuming, and often incomprehensible, especially for full-bloods who could not speak English.[17]

When Agent Ward finally submitted his register of Article 14 claimants to the War Department, he forwarded the names of only sixty-nine heads of families, thirty-nine of whom were mixed-bloods or white men with Choctaw wives.[18] The sworn testimony of many Indians and whites later established the fact that Ward, who was often drunk and had sometimes used pages from his official register as "shaving paper," had been so unyielding in his efforts to rid Mississippi of the Choctaw, especially the full-bloods, that he had often refused or destroyed their applications, had deleted their names from the register after acceptance, and had urged removal agents to whip anyone refusing to emigrate.[19] Although the War Department never condoned these actions, Ward apparently believed that he was carrying out the intent of the federal government. His superiors in Washington were long in contradicting him. Nothing was done to chastise the agent. He was eventually dismissed in November 1833, not because of his scandalous conduct, but because the number of Indians remaining in Mississippi, according to the War Department, was then too small to justify the presence of an agent. Nevertheless, War Department records indicate that several thousand Choctaw remained in the state, and President Jackson insisted that only those whose names appeared on Ward's register were to receive land. Protests from Indians claiming to have rights under Article 14 notwithstanding, Jackson permitted the sale of land in the Choctaw cession.[20]

In the mid-1830s the treaty rights of Choctaw who resisted removal became obscured as a three-cornered battle developed between speculators, settlers, and the Indians. The speculators wanted to acquire title to Indian allotments as cheaply and quickly as possible, while the settlers advocated preemption, the right of squatters to purchase land without competition at a minimum price before it went on sale at public auction. The Choctaw, who were struggling to secure their treaty rights and to acquire land for cultivation, were little match for these two groups. When evidence began to surface that Agent Ward had been willfully obstructive and guilty of misconduct in carrying out the provisions of Article 14, however, anti-Jacksonites rallied to the cause of the harassed Choctaw. Meanwhile the outbreak of Indian-white conflict in Alabama led white Mississippians to flood Congress and the executive department with petitions demanding the immediate removal of all Indians remaining within the state. These factors led Jackson, on his last day in office, to recommend the establishment of a commission to investigate all outstanding claims by the Choctaw still in Mississippi. As criticism from prominent Whig politicians became too strong to ignore, the new administration of Martin Van Buren appointed such a commission. The task determining the validity of claims under Article 14 was legally complex as well as politically sensitive.[21]

The official attitude of the Office of Indian Affairs in Washington toward the Mississippi Choctaw in the 1830s is best indicated by the statistical tables appended to the reports of Commissioner of Indian Affairs Thomas Hartley Crawford. Crawford, an able bureaucrat who served under every president from Martin Van Buren to James K. Polk, listed the Indians under the heading "to be removed." [22] One of the more enlightened men to hold his position during the Jacksonian era, Crawford firmly believed that Indians, "even the moral and educated ones," had nothing to gain from living near whites in organized states of the Union. "Equality he [the Indian] does not, and cannot possess," Crawford argued, "and the influence that is the just possession of his qualities, in the ordinary social relations of life, is denied him." In the West, however, the situation would be far different. There, among his brethren in the relocated Choctaw Nation, "a fair and wide field will be open before him, in which he can cultivate the moral and intellectual virtues of the human beings around him, and aid in elevating them to the highest condition which they are capable of reaching." In the West the Choctaw would enjoy "the pleasures of ancient acquaintances, common habits, and common interests." The removal of all remaining Choctaw was "an event desirable in all aspects of the subject."[23] Although Crawford was a staunch Jacksonian Democrat, his views were shared by the Whig leaders in the Harrison and Tyler administrations.[24]

On August 23, 1842, the Whig-controlled Congress enacted a law providing that all claims under Article 14 had to be submitted for review within one year or would be "forever barred." Since the amount of unsold land in the counties carved from the Choctaw cession was rapidly decreasing, Congress authorized the issuance of scrip certificates in lieu of land to Indians who were identified as having legitimate claims. The scrip would be redeemable at land offices in Mississippi, Louisiana, Alabama, and Arkansas. Two certificates were to be prepared for each award, each good for one half of the land. In order to promote emigration, the second certificate was to be withheld until the Indian claimant arrived in the western Indian Territory.[25] Seeking to rid Mississippi once and for all of what many citizens then identified as "a burdensome population," Whig leaders were as willing as Democrats to ignore the treaty rights of the Mississippi Choctaw.[26]

The general distrust which most Mississippi Choctaw felt toward both Democratic and Whig leaders of the U.S. government by the 1840s is evident in the words spoken in 1843 by Chief Cobb, an Article 14 claimant, to the federal agent in charge of emigration.

> *Brother:* We have heard you talk as from the lips of our father, the great white chief at Washington, and my people have called upon me to speak to you. The red man has no books, and when he wishes to make known his views, like his fathers before him he speaks from his mouth. He is afraid of *writing.* When he *speaks,* he knows what he says; the great spirit hears him. *Writing* is the invention of the pale faces; it gives birth to error and to feuds. The great spirit *talks*—we hear him in the thunder—in the rushing winds, and the mighty water—but he never *writes.*
> *Brother:* When you were young we were strong; we fought by your side; but our arms are now broken. You have grown large. My people have become small.

> *Brother:* My voice is weak; you can scarcely hear me; it is not the shout of a warrior but the wail of an infant. I have lost it in mourning over the misfortunes of my people. These are their graves, and in those aged pines you hear the ghosts of the departed.—Their ashes are here, and we have been left to protect them. Our warriors are nearly all gone to the far country west; but *here* are our dead. Shall we go too, and give their bones to the wolves?
>
> *Brother:* Two sleeps have passed since we heard you talk. We have thought upon it. You ask us to leave our country, and tell us it is our father's wish. We would not desire to displease our father. We respect him, and you his child. But the Choctaw always thinks. We want *time* to answer.
>
> *Brother:* Our hearts are full. Twelve winters ago our chiefs sold our country. Every warrior that you see here was opposed to the treaty. If the dead could have been counted, it could never have been made, but alas! though they stood around, they could not be seen or heard. Their tears came in the raindrops, and their voices in the wailing wind, but the pale faces knew it not, and our land was taken away.
>
> *Brother:* We do not now complain. The Choctaw suffers, but he never weeps. You have the strong arm and we cannot resist. But the pale faces worship the great spirit. So does the red man. The great spirit loves truth. When you took our country, you promised us land. There is your promise in the book. Twelve times have the trees dropped their leaves, and yet we have received no land. Our houses have been taken from us. The white man's plough turns up the bones of our fathers. We dare not kindle our fires; and yet you said we might remain and you would give us land.
>
> *Brother:* Is this truth? But we believe, now our great father knows our condition, he will listen to us. We are as mourning orphans in our country; but our father will take us by the hand. When he fulfills his promise, we will answer his talk. He means well. We know it. But we cannot think now. Grief has made children of us. When our business is settled we shall be men again, and talk to our Great Father about what he has proposed.
>
> *Brother:* You stand in the moccasins of a great chief; you speak the words of a mighty nation, and your talk was long. My people are small; their shadow scarcely reaches to your knee; they are scattered and gone: When I shout I hear my voice in the depths of the woods, but no answering shout comes back. My words, therefore, are few. I have nothing more to say.[27]

Cobb's eloquent rhetoric made little impression on the enrolling agent, who continued to push for the removal of the Choctaw. Although Mississippi newspaper reporters transcribed Cobb's words and reprinted them in their newspapers, readers generally wanted the Indians to find redress for their grievances outside the state. Mississippians with a direct interest in the Choctaw claims, however, sometimes actually hindered the removal process.

The decision to issue scrip certificates to bona fide claimants prompted the emergence of two groups of white speculators in Mississippi. One sought to gain control of the scrip by establishing the legitimacy of Indian claims, and the other planned to obtain the scrip by controlling the removal process to the West. Unless the members of the former group received "just" compensation for their services, they thwarted the removal of the Indians.[28]

By the mid-1840s the entire Choctaw claims issue had become extremely volatile in Mississippi. Whigs and Democrats alike accused each other of speculation, obstructionism, and various misdemeanors. A duel fought in February 1844 over one such accusation led to the death of a Democratic newspaper editor.[29] In September 1845, Jefferson Davis, then a Democratic candidate for Congress, told a political rally at Jackson that the Choctaw claims were "the claims of *white* men" or really "NO CLAIMS AT ALL." In fact, Davis claimed that speculators were actually bringing back Choctaw from Indian Territory and registering them as Article 14 claimants in Mississippi.[30] The heated political controversy over the Choctaw claims in the Magnolia State did not go unnoticed in Washington.

Constant communications from Mississippi politicians, settlers, speculators, and attorneys allegedly representing the interests of Choctaw, and from the Indians themselves, consumed much of Indian Commissioner Crawford's time and energy and only reinforced his conviction that removal of all of the Choctaw from the state was the best solution.[31] One means used to promote the desired exodus was the employment of influential leaders of the western Choctaw Nation. Such prominent and beloved men as Nitakechi, nephew of the famous Chief Pushmataha, accompanied their federal agent to Mississippi in order to encourage their brethren there to emigrate. These efforts met with some success.[32]

Despite the inequities of the arrangement offered by the federal government and the blatant violation of their treaty rights, about 3,500 Indians had accepted the government's terms and had left Mississippi by the end of 1847. Removal to the West, described in favorable terms by Nitakechi and other visiting tribal leaders, seemed preferable to some of the individuals who were reduced to pathetic circumstances in Mississippi. The entry of large numbers of white settlers into the Choctaw cession had reduced the once self-sufficient Indians to an impoverished state. Forced to eke out an existence as squatters or itinerant agricultural workers, and caught between the schemes and counterschemes of white settlers, land speculators, and attorneys—all seeking to profit at their expense—some Choctaw accepted the scrip and headed west.[33]

When the government decided in the summer of 1847 to pay the scrip outside Mississippi, emigration slowed to a trickle, since attorneys who had previously encouraged removal and had converted the scrip to cash for payment of their "fees" in Mississippi now thwarted the removal operations. By 1849, newly appointed Whig Indian Commissioner Orlando Brown was concerned that the expensive removal operations in Mississippi were accomplishing very little. Viewing the operations as "an obligation voluntarily assumed" by the federal government for the "benefit and the advantage" of the state of Mississippi, he predicted that "all that can be induced to go" would leave within a year and suggested that the operations should then cease. "Those that shall then remain," he stated, "would be permitted to do so in the quiet enjoyment of their rights as citizens."[34] Subsequent events proved Brown wrong.

White Mississippians were unrelenting in their efforts to evict the Choctaw despite the cost to the federal government. Jefferson Davis, now a U.S. senator, advised Commissioner Brown in March 1850 that it was "an object of great importance" to his state that the Indians "be removed and prevented from returning." For many years Davis had maintained that some Indians were actually making their way back to Mississippi from Indian Territory.[35] The senator may have been correct. There is disagreement today among scholars, as there was among Davis's contemporaries, regarding the exact number of Choctaw in Mississippi at any time during the antebellum period. Most Mississippi politicians, however, believed that there were too many, regardless of the actual number, and these leaders made repeated efforts to convince the Indian Office that their state should be rid of "the annoyance" of any and all "stragglers."[36]

From the 1830s to the 1850s, every Indian town that had existed in the Choctaw tribal estate before the Treaty of Dancing Rabbit Creek was abandoned. Eventually all or part of twenty-four new countries were formed from the ceded lands.[37] After 1833 the Choctaw in Mississippi were no longer viewed as tribal Indians by the federal government, and the Mississippi Constitution of 1832 empowered the state legislature to admit them to "all the rights and privileges of free white citizens" upon such terms "as the legislature may from time to time deem proper."[38] Some Choctaw, especially highly acculturated mixed-bloods, did subsequently petition and receive citizenship rights from the legislature.[39] Former chieftain Greenwood Leflore, who had received a "special reservation" for supporting the 1830 removal treaty, not only remained in the state but became quite prosperous; he eventually owned 15,000 acres of land and 400 slaves, served two terms in the lower house of the legislature, and spent one term in the senate.[40] Unlike Leflore, however, the vast majority of the Indians, especially the full-bloods, had few, if any, of the rights and privileges enjoyed by white citizens.

Many aspects of the everyday life of the Mississippi Choctaw after 1833 still remain to be investigated, but the evidence seems to indicate that the Indians lived as a marginal group in a rapidly growing society that made rather clear-cut distinctions between whites and blacks. Having suffered at the hands of white settlers, speculators, and attorneys, most of the propertyless Indians avoided extensive contacts with whites by retreating farther and farther into the less desirable heavily forested marginal lands in east central Mississippi. There they eked out a living, occasionally finding employment as itinerant agricultural workers.[41] Observers in the 1840s reported seeing partially clothed Indians "gleaning a precarious subsistence, and enduring too often, in this land of abundance, the pangs of hunger."[42]

Possibly the worst feature of life in Mississippi for many Choctaw after removal was the virtual state of peonage in which they were held by avaricious merchants who furnished them goods at exorbitant prices. Former Congressman John F. H. Claiborne, who headed the commission appointed in 1842 to investigate the Choctaw claims, reported in 1844 that the plight of the Indians was "worse than the subjection of slaves." According to Claiborne, the forms of social control used by whites were numerous. "A complete system of *espionage* is maintained," he noted. Individuals with a speaking knowledge of the Choctaw language were employed to "delude and alarm the Indians." The Choctaw were threatened with fines and imprisonment for real or imaginary infractions of state laws of which they probably had no knowledge. Denied access to either schools or churches and "ignorant of our laws and language, and the extent of their rights," Claiborne contended, the full-bloods were preyed upon by "hungry wolves" whose only concern was to "lap up . . . the last life-blood of a once noble but now miserable race." Although Claiborne's account of the injustices being suffered by the Choctaw under "the Shylock care and stepmother tenderness of speculators" was designed to promote their removal, it is supported by other contemporary accounts.[43]

In 1849, 100 Choctaw living in Jasper and Newton counties, which had been formed from the lands ceded in 1830, reported that they had suffered numerous indignities at the hands of whites seeking to force their removal. "Our tribe has been woefully imposed upon of late," the Indians told an old and trusted white friend, adding, "We have had our habitations torn down and burned; our fences destroyed, cattle turned up into our fields and we ourselves have been scourged, manacled, fettered and otherwise personally abused." These actions were probably intended to effect the departure from Mississippi of acculturated Choctaw who, for one reason or another, had not assimilated into white society. Such Choctaw were undoubtedly a visible and annoying exception to the commonly held stereotype that Indians had no use for good farming land. The victimized Indians of Jasper and Newton counties viewed emigration as preferable to the indignities they had suffered. The treatment afforded these people was an example that was heeded by unacculturated full-blood Indians, who found new reason to retreat even farther into the lands least desired by whites.[44]

In 1851 Joseph Beckham Cobb, a wealthy Whig planter from Noxubee County, where the Treaty of Dancing Rabbit Creek had been negotiated, published a collection of essays and sketches entitled *Mississippi Scenes*. According to Cobb, "the lot and condition" of the Indians was "far more deplorable" than that of the black slaves in his state. "Our conduct, as respects right and justice, humanity and religion, is vastly more to be contemned and reprehended, when viewed in connection with our Indian policy, than in the other case," he asserted, adding, "In a few years more a red man will be a rare sight in the land of his inheritance." Cobb claimed that despite the "halo of romantic and poetic interest" that such writers as James Fenimore

Cooper and Washington Irving had conferred upon the Indians, the "red men" of his day were actually another breed. "The Indians of our day," he wrote, "besides having a full share of all the lower and degrading vices of the Southern negro, such as stealing, lying, and filthy tastes, are noted for cowardice, and craft, and meanness of every description." As far as he was concerned, the Indians did not possess "a single admirable virtue, or magnanimous or noble quality of heart or mind." In fact, Cobb argued, black slaves were superior to Indians in all respects. "I do not know a negro that would countenance an exchange of situations with a Choctaw," he maintained, noting, "as a general thing, these are hardly above animals."[45]

In 1854, three years after the publication of Cobb's book of sketches on southern life, New Englander Frederick Law Olmsted visited Mississippi and saw Indians there firsthand. While Olmsted watched them hoeing cotton, he pondered various differences between these people and blacks. "Niggers are property, the same as horses and cattle," a white planter told him. Itinerant Indians, who were paid fifty cents a day, supposedly "worked well for a few days at a time: [but they] were better at picking than at hoeing." The planter asserted that Indians "don't pick so much in a day as niggers, but do it better." His wife, however, showed general contempt for the Indians and claimed that they were really "good for nothing."[46] Her attitude, like that of Joseph Cobb, undoubtedly reflected majority sentiment in the state. When Indian Agent Douglas H. Cooper visited Mississippi in 1856 at the request of the western Choctaw Nation to determine the number of Indians still there, he reported that, "although some of them are nominally citizens, they are all in a very hopeless and degraded condition."[47] By the eve of the American Civil War, most Mississippi Choctaw were living a bleak life as squatters on the most marginal and isolated lands, with a white population encircling them. Denied their treaty rights and only nominally citizens of the state, they steadfastly held on to the last remnants of their traditional way of life and minimized their contacts with whites. Only a few highly acculturated mixed-bloods were ever assimilated into white society.[48]

During the Civil War, federal relations with the Mississippi Choctaw came to a virtual standstill. At least one acculturated mixed-blood, former Chief Greenwood Leflore, remained loyal to the Union and suffered heavy property losses as a result.[49] Some 180 Choctaw men living in the counties carved out of the 1830 land cession were mustered into the service of the Confederacy in 1862. Their unit, the First Mississippi Choctaw Infantry Battalion, was trained and led by whites and was assigned to the Department of Mississippi and Eastern Louisiana under Lieutenant-General John C. Pemberton. The entire battalion was surrounded and captured while it trained at Camp Moore in Louisiana in 1863 during the Vicksburg campaign. The fate of these soldiers remains a mystery, but their kinfolk in Mississippi assumed that they had been sent to the West. The loss of so large a number of men, together with the turmoil and disruption of the war and Reconstruction, undoubtedly encouraged the Choctaw to remain as inconspicuous as possible.[50]

After the Civil War, the federal government renewed its effort to entice the Mississippi Choctaw to resettle in the West. In 1866 a Reconstruction treaty was forced upon the western Choctaw Nation, which had been in the vanguard of the secessionist movement in the Indian Territory. This treaty included a provision calling for the allotment in severalty of tribal lands if approved by the Choctaw council. Government officials and many well-intentioned though seriously misguided humanitariaan reformers had long argued that the conversion of communally owned tribal lands into private property would be an important step in the transformation of the Indians into "civilized" Americans. Under the treaty allotment provision, the so-called absent Choctaw in Mississippi were eligible to participate in the division of the tribal estate if they became bona fide residents of the western nation. In order to encourage their participation, the United States promised to publish notices advertising this treaty provision in Mississippi newspapers.[51] Possibly because of the strong opposition to allotment among the western Choctaw, the Indian Office never published the notices. It is interesting to note, however, that a small-scale movement of Mississippi Choctaw to the West took place in 1866 and continued even after the Choctaw Nation had officially rejected the allotment scheme in 1870.[52] This activity had more to do with events in Mississippi than with the treaty of 1866.

Between 1865 and 1890, Mississippi underwent considerable social and political change.[53] The Choctaw, neither black nor white in a state where tensions between those races were at an all-time high, tried to avoid conflict by keeping to themselves. A few joined their brethren in the West, possibly enticed to do so by kinfolk already there, but most simply retreated farther into their dismal haunts. In the late 1870s and in the 1880s, however, white landowners increasingly sought additional land for cultivation, and even the marginal lands of the Choctaw were brought into production. At the same time, the exodus of emancipated blacks from the east central portion of the state to the rapidly expanding plantations of the delta region created an acute labor shortage. These two events contributed to the transformation of the Choctaw from squatters into sharecroppers.[54]

Since the Indians stood almost entirely outside the monetary system of the dominant society, they made the transition to becoming sharecroppers with relative ease, inasmuch as they could now receive food rations and others supplies in return for their labor. In fact the sharecropping system actually created some new opportunities for the Choctaw who were able to participate, although in a very limited way, in the economy of the larger society without totally sacrificing their ethnic identity. The sharecropping system kept the Indians in a virtual state of debt peonage, but Choctaw schools and churches did emerge in the sharecropping communities. The establishment of these institutions was the most momentous event in the history of the Mississippi Choctaw since the disruption caused by the Treaty of Dancing Rabbit Creek.[55] Despite the provisions of the 1868 and 1890 state constitutions, which left "Indians not taxed" (together with "idiots and insane persons") disenfranchised, and despite the poor living, working, and health conditions they endured, Choctaw sharecroppers began developing a new sense of community in the late nineteenth century as a result of their schools and churches.[56]

Choctaw from Indian Territory played a role in the cultural reawakening that took place in Mississippi. Aroused by reports of the poor conditions among their eastern brethren, western Choctaw missionaries went east.[57] In 1889 the Choctaw Nation petitioned Congress to assist in promoting the emigration of eastern Choctaw to Indian Territory, and the tribal council sent its own delegation to Mississippi in 1891 to encourage such activity. The Choctaw Nation's financial support of emigrants and its readiness to grant citizenship to the newcomers waned rapidly in the mid-1890s, however, when federal officials began intensive efforts to accomplish by statute what the United States had failed to secure by treaty in 1866.[58]

In 1893 Congress made the Choctaw Nation subject to the provisions of the General Allotment Act of 1887. This legislation, popularly known as the Dawes act, called for the allotment in severalty of tribal lands. It was supported by a group of humanitarian reformers, generally referred to as "Friends of the Indian," who wanted to detribalize the Indians in order to transform them into mirror images of American farmers, as well as by other Americans who were more interested in acquiring Indian land than in promoting Indian "civilization."[59] Despite strong Choctaw opposition to any division of their tribal land, Congress enacted legislation in 1896 directing the Dawes commission to prepare the final citizenship rolls.[60]

The federal government's decision to force the allotment policy upon the Choctaw in Indian Territory awakened the spirit of free enterprise among many expectant capitalists. As a federal judge later remarked, "attorneys at law, farmers, merchants, bankers, a preacher, and others without any settled vocation in life" suddenly became staunch supporters of the rights of the descendants of Article 14 claimants in Mississippi.[61] Two such individuals, attorneys Robert L. Owen and Charles F. Winton, solicited contracts from Indians which included provisions for fees totaling 50 percent of the claims of their clients.[62] These attorneys were thwarted, however, by the Dawes commission, which had been empowered in 1896 to determine the validity of citizenship claims. The commissioners consistently ruled that anyone claiming citizenship rights as a Mississippi Choctaw had to settle in Indian Territory and prove descent from a relative who had attempted to comply with the provisions of Article 14.[63] When the Dawes commission rejected a large group of claimants represented by Owen on these grounds, he appealed to a U.S. court in Indian Territory. The court's decision in 1897 that removal was necessary to file for Choctaw citizenship failed to convince Owen, who, together with Winton, began lobbying in Congress for a more liberal interpretation of the rights of Mississippi Choctaw who did not want to leave the state. Their efforts convinced Congressman John Sharp Williams, whose district included a large number of these Choctaw, that Choctaw rights were being abridged.[64]

Between the summer of 1897 and the closing of the tribal citizenship rolls in 1907, Williams and other members of the Mississippi congressional delegation used their oratorical and parliamentary skills to defend the rights of the Mississippi Choctaw to a share in the division of the western tribal estate. Attorneys Winton and Owen also continued to press the claims of their clients. Their lobbying effort awakened additional congressional interest in the Mississippi Choctaw, even though it failed to bring the lobbyists what they wanted for themselves.[65]

In the late 1890s and early 1900s, Congress enacted several measures pertaining to the Mississippi Choctaw. In June 1898 the Curtis act authorized the Dawes commission to question witnesses under oath in order to identify Article 14 claimants or their descendants.[66] When a field party arrived in Mississippi in 1899, it discovered that most full-bloods were reluctant to testify, fearing that they would be forced to emigrate.[67] In 1902, to facilitate removal of the full-bloods, Congress ruled that "Choctaw blood" was a sufficient test and that full-bloods would not have to prove ancestry dating back to Article 14 registrants or to people who had attempted to register in the 1830s.[68] Although the would-be claimants before the commission included more indigent whites and blacks than Indians, about 300 full-bloods were eventually identified and removed at government expense to Indian Territory in 1903.[69] Many others were brought west by speculators, but in order to protect such emigrants, Congress had thoughtfully acted in 1900 to invalidate all prior liens upon their property in Indian Territory.[70]

By the time the official Choctaw Nation rolls were ordered closed on March 4, 1907, some 25,000 persons had applied for identification as Mississippi Choctaw, but fewer than, 1,700 had been accepted. Thousands of whites, blacks, and mixed-bloods had been denied identification.[71] The closing of the rolls was challenged by many petitions from alleged Mississippi Choctaw or from lawyers claiming to represent them.[72] During the years preceding World War I, members of the Mississippi congressional delegation defended the right of the Choctaw in their state to share in the wealth of the Choctaw Nation and sought to secure legislation to reopen the rolls. [73] The congressional delegation from Oklahoma, which had been admitted to statehood on November 16, 1907, vigorously opposed the Mississippians, claiming, with a good deal of justification, that their actions would benefit only white attorneys seeking to use the Mississippi Choctaw for their own purposes. [74] In 1908 the Choctaw council had warned that many non-Choctaw, including "Mexicans, Creoles, Dagoes, and Indians of other tribes," were claiming to be Choctaw in order to obtain a portion of the tribal funds that still remained after allotment. [75] The Choctaw Nation was ably defended by its attorney, Patrick J. Hurley, who argued that the so-called friends of the Mississippi Choctaw were the same individuals who had reduced them to "a state that is almost peonage" and had "in practice" denied them the right of citizenship granted them under Mississippi laws. [76]

On May 18, 1916, the Oklahoma delegation was able to secure congressional enactment of a final per capita payment to the western Choctaw that made no provision for the enrollment of additional Mississippi Choctaw or for their inclusion in the distribution. [77] The nine-year-long struggle to reopen the rolls, however, had focused attention on the condition of the Choctaw in Mississippi.

In March 1917 a congressional investigating team traveled to the state to review the plight of the Choctaw at the request of Mississippi Congressman William Venable of Meridian. Venable assured the Indians through an interpreter, "This is not a committee with any purpose to take you to Oklahoma or anything of that kind. This committee wants to find out your condition so that on their report, if the American Congress sees fit it can do the Indians some good and give them some benefit here in Mississippi."[78]

The committee members heard a distressing report. Despite the land allotment provisions of the 1830 removal treaty, the Choctaw owned little, if any, land. Those who did own land, moreover, had the poorest in the region. Many Choctaw lived in small, starkly furnished and poorly ventilated cabins as sharecroppers. Kept in a state of indebtedness, they were unable to "pay off the furnish" to white planters. When Congressman Patrick Norton of North Dakota asked full-blood Olmon Cumby of Carthage whether the Choctaw needed protection from some of the white people in the community, he was told that "them that wears fine collars is going to beat you every time." Illiterate in English, disenfranchised by their inability to pay the poll tax, ill clothed and ill fed, and in many instances, suffering from tuberculosis, the Choctaw nevertheless demonstrated little interest in leaving Mississippi. When one congressman persisted in asking why, a Choctaw sharecropper replied, "This is my native home."[79]

In May 1918, as a result of the congressional investigation in Mississippi and the ravages of an influenza epidemic which had killed one of every five Choctaw there, Congress appropriated funds for the relief and education of these Indians. Commissioner of Indian Affairs Cato Sells personally visited the Choctaw "in their homes, at work, on their sick beds, and in their varied relationships of life." Sells advised Secretary of the Interior Franklin K. Lane and President Woodrow Wilson, "It is apparent that the Oklahoma rolls have been finally closed against the Mississippi Choctaws, and that their future is in Mississippi, where, everything considered, I am persuaded that these deserving people should receive kind, prompt, and substantial consideration from the Government." The agency established by the Wilson administration at Philadelphia in Neshoba County offered the Choctaw medical, educational, and economic assistance. Farmland was purchased for Indian use.[80] To the Choctaw who had remained steadfast in their refusal to abandon their homeland, and to their sons or grandsons returning home after service in the armed forces of the United States during World War I, these congressional actions were "the first real sign of positive federal interest since 1830."[81]

The federal government's "rediscovery" of the rights of the Mississippi Choctaw in Mississippi after an eighty-five-year effort to evict them from the state marked the beginning of a series of events which culminated in the establishment of a reservation in 1944 and the reestablishment of tribal government the following year. Organized as the Mississippi Band of Choctaw Indians in 1945, the Mississippi Choctaw subsequently dedicated themselves, as had their ancestors, to the perpetuation of their tribal heritage and the improvement of their living and working conditions in the state.[82] Conclusive judicial recognition of the Mississippi Band as a tribe and its lands as "Indian Country" came in June 1978, when in *United States v. John*, the U.S. Supreme Court ruled that the Mississippi Band possessed the degree of sovereignty that had been allowed to other federally recognized tribes.[83] Today, proud of their strides toward self-government and toward the preservation of their culture, the Mississippi Choctaw proudly proclaim, "Chahta Hapia Hoke"—"We are Choctaw"—and endeavor to live in their ancestral homeland in the quiet enjoyment of their rights as Choctaw citizens.[84]

Notes

1. For the dimensions of the current debate on Jackson's relations with the southern tribes, see Francis Paul Prucha, "Andrew Jackson's Indian Policy: A Reassessment," *Journal of American History* 56 (December 1969): 527–39; Ronald N. Satz, *American Indian Policy in the Jacksonian Era* (Lincoln: University of Nebraska Press, 1975); Michael Paul Rogin, *Fathers and Children: Andrew Jackson and the Subjugation of the American Indian* (New York: Knopf, 1975); Robert V. Remini, *Andrew Jackson*, 3 vols. (New York: Harper and Row, 1977–84), 1:321–98, 2:257–79, 3:293–314.

2. An excellent introduction to this subject is Walter L. Williams, ed., *Southeastern Indians since the Removal Era* (Athens: University of Georgia Press, 1979).

3. Anthropologist John H. Peterson, Jr., asserts in "Three Efforts at Development among the Choctaws of Mississippi," in ibid., "The Mississippi Choctaws have been almost completely ignored by students of the American Indian" (p. 142). Edward Davis, in "The Mississippi Choctaws," *Chronicles of Oklahoma* 10 (June 1932):257–66, presents a brief survey of federal relations with these Indians, but there are gaps as well as errors of fact and problems of interpretation in his essay. Neither the standard history of the Choctaw (Angie Debo, *The Rise and Fall of the Choctaw Republic*, 2d ed. [(Norman: University of Oklahoma Press, 1961]) nor the recent attempt to update it (Jesse O. McKee and Jon A. Schlenker, *The Choctaws: Cultural Evolution of a Native American Tribe* [Jackson: University Press of Mississippi, 1980]) provides a detailed analysis of the relations between the Mississippi Choctaw and the federal government after removal. A useful guide to the literature on these Indians is Clara Sue Kidwell and Charles Roberts, *The Choctaws: A Critical Bibliography* (Bloomington: Indiana University Press for the Newberry Library, 1980), 61–68.

4. Debo, *The Rise and Fall of the Choctaw Republic*, 24–57; Arthur H. DeRosier, Jr., *The Removal of the Choctaw Indians* (Knoxville: University of Tennessee Press, 1970), v–vi, 164; *National Banner and Nashville Whig*, May 27, 1830; Satz, *American Indian Policy*, 67–69; Jackson to the Senate, May 6,1830, in James D. Richardson, comp., *A Compilation of the Messages and Papers of the Presidents*, 10 vols. (Washington, D.C.: Government Printing Office, 1896–99), 2:479 (quotation); Charles J. Kappler, comp. and ed., *Indian Affairs: Laws and Treaties*, 4 vols. (Washington, D.C.: Government Printing Office, 1904–29), 2:310–19.

5. Satz, *American Indian Policy*, 39–44, 69; Richard B. Latner, *The Presidency of Andrew Jackson: White House Politics, 1829–1837* (Athens: University of Georgia Press, 1979), 94–98. In the introduction to his edition of Jeremiah Evarts, *Cherokee Removal: The "William Penn" Essays and other Writings* (Knoxville: University of Tennessee Press, 1979), Francis Paul Prucha asserts that the removal issue was "a question that agitated the nation to its very roots, in the press and on the floor of Congress, and it touched the fundamental conception of the United States as a Christian nation" (p. 3). Robert V. Remini, however, in *Andrew Jackson* claims that "there was not public outcry against it. In fact it was hardly noticed" (2:265).

6. For Eaton's role in the negotiations, see *Journal of Proceedings at the Treaty of*

From the Removal Treaty Onward

Dancing Rabbit Creek, September 15–28, 1830, in *Correspondence on the Subject of the Emigration of Indians*, S. Doc. 512, 23d Cong., 1st sess., 2:251–63; John Coffee to Jackson, September 29,1830, in *Correspondence of Andrew Jackson*, ed. John Spencer Bassett, 7 vols. (Washington, D.C.: Carnegie Institution, 1926–35), 4:180; *Arkansas Advocate*, October 29, 1830; *Niles' Weekly Register* 38 (October 23, 1830):140, 39 (November 6, 1830):182–83. Since the Removal Act had passed the Senate by a vote of 28 to 19 (a smaller proportion than the two-thirds necessary for ratification of treaties) and the House by vote of 102 to 97 (a narrow margin, indeed), it was essential that the administration convince Congress of the merit of this first treaty submitted under the Removal Act. For the debates on the Removal Act, see U.S. Congress, *Register of Debates*, 21st Cong., 1st sess., 305ff., 58off. (February 24, 1830, and following in the House, and April 6,1830, and following in the Senate). The Choctaw treaty was ratified by the Senate (35 to 12) in February 1831, but the preamble, which stated that President Jackson was unable to protect the Choctaw from the operation of the laws of Mississippi, was stricken. See note 9.

    7. Kappler, *Indian Affairs*, 2:313–18. Because of its centrality to the issue of the rights of the Mississippi Choctaw after removal, I quote Article 14 in its entirety: "Each Choctaw head of a family being desirous to remain and become a citizen of the States, shall be permitted to do so, by signifying his intention to the Agent within six months from the ratification of his Treaty, and he or she shall thereupon be entitled to a reservation of one section of six hundred and forty acres of land, to be bounded by sectional lines of survey; in like manner shall be entitled to one half that quantity for each unmarried child which is living with him over ten years of age; and a quarter section to such child as may be under 10 years of age, to adjoin the location of the parent. If they reside upon said lands intending to become citizens of the States for five years after the ratification of this Treaty, in that case a grant in fee simple shall issue; said reservation shall include the present improvement of the head of the family, or a portion of it. Persons who claim under this article shall not lose the privilege of a Choctaw citizen, but if they ever remove are not to be entitled to any portion of the Choctaw annuity" (p. 313).

    8. *Journal of Proceedings at the Treaty of Dancing Rabbit Creek*, S.Doc.512,p. 259; Mary E. Young, *Redskins, Ruffleshirts, and Rednecks: Indian Allotments in Alabama and Mississippi, 1830–1860* (Norman: University of Oklahoma Press, 1961), 50–51. As late as mid-1831, Eaton maintained that the allotment provisions of the treaty would not impede the government's removal effort. See Eaton to Major F. W. Armstrong, April 26, 1831, Records of the Office of Indian Affairs, Letters Sent, 7: 200, Record Group 75, National Archives, Washington, D.C. (hereafter cited as ROIA, LS or LR [Letters Received], RG 75, NA).

    9. *Journal of Proceedings at the Treaty of Dancing Rabbit Creek*, S.Doc.512, pp. 256–61. For criticism of Eaton's handling of the negotiations, see *New York Observer*, October 30, 1830; *New York Daily Advertiser*, quoted in *Nashville Republican and State Gazette*, November 13, 1830. Eaton inserted the following preamble in the Choctaw treaty, which was stricken from the documents as ratified by the Senate: "WHEREAS the General Assembly of the State of Mississippi has extended the laws of said State to persons and property within the chartered limits of the same, and the President of the United States has said that he cannot protect the Choctaw people from the operation of these laws; Now therefore that the Choctaw may live under their own laws in peace with the United States and the State of Mississippi they have determined to sell their lands east of the Mississippi and have accordingly agreed to the following articles of treaty" (Kappler, *Indian Affairs*, 2:310–11; U.S. Congress, *Register of Debates*, 21st Cong., 2d sess., 346–48).

    10. According to Wilcomb E. Washburn, *Red Man's Land—White Man's Law: A Study of the Past and Present Status of the American Indian* (New York: Scribner's, 1971), "the principal point of dispute between white and Indian historically has been land. The

greatest leagl gap between the two cultures has been the respective attitudes toward that commodity" (p. 143). In her perceptive article "Indian Removal and Land Allotment: The Civilized Tribes and Jacksonian Justice" (*American Historical Review* 64 [October 1958], Mary E. Young notes that "nearly all the Indians had some experience in trade, but to most of them the conception of land as a salable commodity was foreign. They had little notion of the exact meaning of an 'acre' or the probable value of their allotments. The government confused them still further by parceling out the lands according to Anglo-American, rather than aboriginal notions of family structure and land ownership" (p. 40).

11. Dorothy V. Jones, *License for Empire: Colonialism by Treaty in Early America* (Chicago: University of Chicago Press, 1982), xii.

12. Satz, *American Indian Policy*, 70–71.

13. Estimates of the number of Choctaw removed and remaining behind vary in the numerous contemporary and secondary accounts. The figure cited above is based on the extensive analysis of many federal government reports provided in *Memorial of the Choctaw Nation*, 42d Cong., 3d sess., February 13, 1873, H. Misc. Doc. 94, pp. 6–11. Also see note 36.

14. Satz, *American Indian Policy*, 84, 178–200; Franklin L. Riley, "Choctaw Land Claims," *Publications of the Mississippi Historical Society* 8 (1904):346–48.

15. Eaton to Ward, November 13, 1830, 23d Cong., 1st sess., S. Doc. 512, 2:42–43; *Memorial of the Choctaw Nation*, H. Misc. Doc. 94, p. 6; Satz, *American Indian Policy*, 83–84; Young, *Redskins, Ruffleshirts, and Rednecks*, 47–72; Grant Foreman, *Indian Removal: The Emigration of the Five Civilized Tribes of Indians*, new ed. (Norman: University of Oklahoma Press, 1953), 31; Riley, "Choctaw Land Claims," 346–47.

16. Franklin E. Plummer to Lewis Cass, May 22, 1832, Cass to Plummer, May 23, 1832, 23d Cong., 1st sess., S. Doc. 512, 2:837–38 (quotation), 3:361–62.

17. Campbell to Cass, August 5, 1832, William Armstrong to George Gibson, October 13, 1832, ibid., 1:386, 3:416–18 (quotation).

18. *American State Papers: Public Lands*, 8 vols. (Washington, D.C.: Gales and Seaton, 1832–61), 8:686 (hereafter cited as ASP: PL); John H. Peterson, Jr., "The Mississippi Band of Choctaw Indians: Their Recent History and Current Social Relations" (Ph.d. diss., University of Georgia, 1970), 19.

19. See the various depositions in the Records of Claims Commissions, Choctaw Removal Records, RG 75, NA; Riley, "Choctaw Land Claims," 346–48.

20. D. Kurtz to Ward, November 5, 1832, Kurtz to William Armstrong, November 5, 1832, ROIA, LS, 9:346–47, RG 75, NA; Young, *Redskins, Ruffleshirts, and Rednecks*, 52–53 (also see p. 57 for a useful map of public land sales in the Choctaw cession between 1833 and 1846).

21. ASP: PL, 8:432–33; David Dickson, J. F. H. Claiborne, Jno. Black, R. J. Walker, and F. S. Lyon to Cass, May 7, 1836, in *Letter from the Secretary of War Relative to the Contracts for the Emigration of the Choctaw Indians*, 28th Cong., 2d sess., H. Doc. 107, p. 6; John Bell, *Report on Land Claims, etc. under the Fourteenth Article Choctaw Treaty*, 24th Cong., 1st sess., May 11, 1836, Rept. 663, pp. 1–10; Commissioner of Indian Affairs Carey A. Harris to Secretary of War Joel R. Poinsett, December 16, 1837, in *Message from the President . . . in Relation to . . . the Treaty of 1830*, 25th Cong., 2d sess., S. Doc. 25, p. 2. There were 1,349 claims under the legislation governing this commission. The commissioners reported on only 261. Of these, 165 were allowed, 65 rejected, 26 recommended for favorable consideration, and 5 left unfinished. See Commissioner of Indian Affairs William Medill to Secretary of War William L. Marcy, April 25, 1846, in *Message from the President . . . Relative to . . . the Choctaw Treaty*, 29th Cong., 1st sess., H. Exec. Doc. 189, p. 2. For the situation in Alabama, see Kenneth L. Valliere, "The Creek War of 1836: A Military History," *Chronicles of Oklahoma* 57 (Winter 1979–80):463–85.

22. Commissioner of Indian Affairs, *Report*, 24th Cong., 2d sess., December 1, 1836,

S. Doc. 1, p. 414; Commissioner of Indian Affairs, *Report*, 26th Cong., 1st sess., November 25, 1839, S. Doc. 1, p. 352. On Crawford's role in shaping federal Indian policy, see Ronald N. Satz, "Thomas Hartley Crawford, 1838–45," in *The Commissioners of Indian Affairs, 1824–1977*, ed. Robert M. Kvasnicka and Herman J. Viola (Lincoln: University of Nebraska Press, 1979), 23–27.

23. Commissioner of Indian Affairs, *Report*, 25th Cong., 3d sess., November 25, 1838, S. Doc. 1, pp. 440–41, 444.

24. Secretary of War John C. Spencer to J. T. Moorehead, March 9, 1842, 27th Cong., 2d sess., in *Letter . . . in Relation to the Adjustment of Claims . . . with the Choctaw Indians*, S. Doc. 188, pp. 2–3; Secretary of War William Wilkins to J. J. McKay, January 21, 1845, 28th Cong., 2d sess., H. Doc. 107, pp. 1–5.

25. *U.S. Statutes at Large* (Boston: Little, Brown and Co., 1856), 5:513–16. The government's handling of the scrip payments was later criticized by the Choctaw Nation; see, for example, Choctaw Nation, *Memorandum of Particulars in Which the Choctaw Nation and Individuals Are Entitled to Relief and Compensation in Case They Are Not Paid the New Proceeds of Their Lands Ceded by the Treaty of September 27, 1830* (Washington, D.C.: Gideon, 1856), 12–18.

26. Spencer to Moorehead, March 16, 1842, 27th Cong., 2d sess., S. Doc. 188, p. 3.

27. Quoted in *Niles' National Register* 64 (April 29, 1843):131–32.

28. Young, *Redskins, Ruffleshirts, and Rednecks*, 62–72. Secretary of War William Wilkins prepared a lengthy summary of the history of the Choctaw claims controversy for President Tyler in 1844; see Wilkins to Tyler, December 7, 1844, Records of the Secretary of War, Letters Sent to the President, 4:210–30, RG 107, NA. W. David Baird describes the activities of an influential western Choctaw who was associated with both groups of speculators in his *Peter Pitchlynn: Chief of the Choctaws* (Norman: University of Oklahoma Press, 1972), 76–79.

29. George Dewey Harmon, *Sixty Years of Indian Affairs: Political, Economic, and Diplomatic, 1789–1850* (Chapel Hill: University of North Carolina Press, 1941), 249–55; James T. McIntosh, ed., *The Papers of Jefferson Davis*, vol. 2: *June 1841–July 1846* (Baton Rouge: Louisiana State University Press, 1974), 29 n. 17, 258, 261 n. 27, 300–1 n. 31; *Vicksburg Sentinel*, March 1, 1844.

30. Speech by Jefferson Davis, September 2, 1845, in McIntosh, *The Papers of Jefferson Davis*, 325.

31. For Crawford's reaction to the "tedious and embarrassing class of business" resulting from the Choctaw claims cases, see Commissioner of Indian Affairs, *Report*, 30th Cong., 2d sess., November 30, 1848, S. Exec. Doc. 1, p. 405. Before his appointment as Indian commissioner, Crawford had served on the commission that investigated alleged frauds committed by white speculators against the Creeks in Alabama. His final report had strongly condemned the numerous frauds perpetrated against these Indians. See Satz, "Thomas Hartley Crawford," 23.

32. See ROIA, LR, Choctaw Agency Emigration, microcopy M-234, roll 185, RG 75, NA; *Arkansas Intelligencer*, December 27, 1845.

33. Commissioner of Indian Affairs, *Report*, 30th Cong., 1st sess., November 30, 1847, S. Exec. Doc. 1, pp. 737–38; Commissioner of Indian Affairs, *Report*, 30th Cong., 2d sess., November 30, 1848, S. Exec. Doc. 1, p. 395. Commissioner of Indians Affairs, *Report*, 31st Cong., 1st sess., November 30, 1849, S. Exec. Doc. 1, p. 948. Under the 1842 legislation and as a result of the findings of the commission that investigated claims under Article 14 during 1837 and 1838, 143 heads of families and their children received land, while 1,150 Choctaw and their 2,683 children became entitled to payment in scrip (Young, *Redskins, Ruffleshirts, and Rednecks*, 65). For a vivid portrayal of conditions in Mississippi in the early 1840s, see J. F. H. Claiborne, *Memorial*, 28th Cong., 1st sess., February 19, 1844, H. Doc. 137.

34. Memorandum from Polk, September 25, 1847, Medill to Samuel M. Rutherford,

October 9, 1847, February 12, 1848, Medill to William L. Marcy, February 11, 1848, all in Commissioner of Indian Affairs, *Report*, 30th Cong., 2d sess., November 30, 1848, S. Exec. Doc. 1, pp. 405, 411–18; Commissioner of Indian Affairs, *Report*, 31st Cong., 1st sess., November 30, 1849, S. Exec. Doc. 1, 948.

35. Davis to Brown, March 27, 1850, ROIA, LR, Choctaw Agency Emigration, microcopy M-234, roll 187, frame 21, RG 75, NA. Also see D. W. Haley to Davis, March 8, 1850, ibid., frames 23–25.

36. See note 13; McKee and Schlenker, *The Choctaws*, 96; Peterson, "The Mississippi Band of Choctaw Indians,": 24–25. Scholarly estimates of the number of Choctaw remaining in the state range from a low of 2,000 to a high of nearly 7,000. See Kidwell and Roberts, *The Choctaws*, 61, and Foreman, *Indian Removal*, 102. For evidence indicating that Indians were returning to Mississippi in the mid-1850s, see Douglas H. Cooper to Charles W. Dean, August 28, 1855, in Commissioner of Indian Affairs, *Report for 1855* (Washington, D.C.: A. O. P. Nicholson, 1856), 152.

37. Charlie M. Beckett, "Choctaw Indians in Mississippi Since 1830" (master's thesis, Oklahoma Agricultural and Mechanical College, 1949), 13.

38. Francis Newton Thorpe, *The Federal and State Constitutions*, 7 vols. (Washington, D.C.: Government Printing Office, 1909), 4:2062.

39. See, for example, Mississippi, *Session Acts*, 19th sess. (February 25, 1836): 56, 420.

40. Florence Rebecca Ray, *Chieftain Greenwood Leflore and the Choctaw Indians of the Mississippi Valley: Last Chief of Choctaws East of Mississippi River*, 2d ed. (Memphis: C. A. Davis, 1936), 58, 61, 71, 73.

41. Peterson, "The Mississippi Band of Choctaw Indians," 21–53.

42. J. F. H. Claiborne, *Memorial*, 28th Cong., 1st sess., February 19, 1844, H. Doc. 137, p. 4.

43. Ibid., 1–6.

44. Petition of One Hundred Red Men, December 6, 1849, ROIA, LR, Choctaw Emigration, RG 75, NA; Peterson, "The Mississippi Band of Choctaw Indians,: 25–27.

45. Joseph B. Cobb, *Mississippi Scenes; or, Sketches of Southern and Western Life and Adventure, Humorous, Satirical, and Descriptive, Including the Legend of Black Creek* (Philadelphia: A. Hart, 1851), 158–59, 177–78.

46. Frederick Law Olmsted, *A Journey in the Back Country* (1860; reprint, New York: Schocken Books, 1970), 173–74.

47. Commissioner of Indian Affairs, *Report*, 34th Cong., 2d sess., November 22, 1856, S. Exec. Doc. 1, p 564. Cooper was in Mississippi preparing a census of the Choctaw there; see Census Roll, 1856, ROIA, Choctaw Removal Records, RG 75, NA. Davis, in "Mississippi Choctaws," 259, assumes that Cooper never made the enumeration as requested by the western Choctaw council.

48. Peterson, "The Mississippi Band of Choctaw Indians," 25.

49. *Petition of John D. Leflore and James C. Harris, Executors of the Last Will and Testament of Greenwood Leflore*, 43d Cong., 1st sess., April 29, 1874, S. Rept. 314, pp. 1–11; Ray, *Chieftain Greenwood Leflore*, 74–79.

50. U.S. War Department, *The War of the Rebellion: A Compilation of the Official Records of the Union and Confederate Armies*, 70 vols. in 128 (Washington, D.C.: Government Printing Office, 1880–1901), ser. 1, 15:286; 24, pt. 3:647, 707; A. J. Brown, *History of Newton County, Mississippi, from 1834 to 1894* (Jackson: Clairon-Ledger, 1894), 96–97; William F. Amann, ed., *Personnel of the Civil War*, vol. 1: *The Confederate Armies* (New York: Thomas Yoseloff, 1961), 30; Ezra J. Warner, *Generals in Gray: Lives of the Confederate Commanders* (Baton Rouge: Louisiana State University Press, 1959), 232–33; Peterson, "The Mississippi Band of Choctaw Indians," 50–52.

51. Kappler, *Indian Affairs*, 2:918–31. Confederate Commissioner of Indian Affairs S. S. Scott advised Secretary of War James Seddon on January 12, 1863, that "the

Choctaws alone, of all the Indian Nations, have remained perfectly united in their loyalty to this Government;" see U.S. War Department, *The War of the Rebellion*, ser. 4, 2:353. The policy of individualizing Indian land tenure by allotment of lands in severalty was long a basic principle of government officials and so-called friends of the Indian. See William T. Hagan, "Private Property: The Indian's Door to Civilization," *Ethnohistory* 3 (Spring 1956):126–37. The 1866 treaty was forced upon both the Choctaw and the Chickasaw. Regarding the relations between these tribes, see Arrell M. Gibson, *The Chickasaws* (Norman: University of Oklahoma Press, 1971); Debo, *The Rise and Fall of the Choctaw Republic*.

52. House Committee on Indian Affairs, *Hearings before the Subcommittee . . . on the Subject of Enrollment in the Five Civilized Tribes* (Washington, D.C.: Government Printing Office, 1915), 9 (hereafter cited as *House Hearings on Enrollment*); Captain George T. Olmsted to E. S. Parker, September 15, 1870, in Commissioner of Indian Affairs *Report* (Washington, D.C.: Government Printing Office, 1870), 291; Choctaw and Chickasaw nations, *Memorial of the Choctaw and Chickasaw Nations Relative to the Rights of the Mississippi Choctaws* (Washington, D.C.: n.p., 1913), 8; Arrell M. Gibson, "The Indians of Mississippi," in *A History of Mississippi*, ed. Richard Aubrey McLemore, 2 vols. (Hattiesburg: University and College Press of Mississippi, 1973), 1:39.

53. Historians John K. Bettersworth, William C. Harris, David G. Sansing, and James G. Revels explore various aspects of this period in separate essays in McLemore, *A History of Mississippi*, 1:542–639.

54. Peterson, "Three Efforts at Development among the Choctaws of Mississippi," 147; Bobby Thompson and John H. Peterson, Jr., "Mississippi Choctaw Identity: Genesis and Change," in *The New Ethnicity: Perspectives from Ethnology*, ed. John W. Bennett (St. Paul: West, 1975), 180–82. For developments among Mississippi's black population, see Vernon Lane Wharton, *The Negro in Mississippi, 1865–1890* (Chapel Hill: University of North Carolina Press, 1947).

55. Peterson, "The Mississippi Band of Choctaw Indians," 48–89.

56. Thorpe, *The Federal and State Constitutions*, 4:2079, 2120; House, Committee on Investigation of the Indian Service, *Hearings*, vol. 2: *Condition of the Mississippi Choctaws* (Washington, D.C.: Government Printing Office, 1917), hereafter cited as *House Hearings on Condition of the Mississippi Choctaws*.

57. Eugene I. Farr, "Religious Assimilation: A Case Study—The Adoption of Christianity by the Choctaw Indians of Mississippi" (Th.D. diss., New Orleans Baptist Theological Seminary, 1948), 28–30; Peterson, "The Mississippi Band of Choctaw Indians," 66–68, 74.

58. Choctaw and Chickasaw nations, *Memorial*, 8, 32–38; A. R. Durant, comp., *Constitution and Laws of the Choctaw Nation* (Dallas: John F. Worley, 1894), 315, 320, 323; Choctaw Nation, *Acts and Resolutions of the General Council . . . Passed at Its Regular Session, October, 1897* (n.p.: Elevator Job Office, 1897), 30–32; *Estate of Charles F. Winton and Others v. Jack Amos and Others, Known as the "Mississippi Choctaw,"* 51 U.S. Court of Claims, No. 29821, 288 (1916), hereafter cited as *Winton v. Amos*.

59. Commissioner to the Five Civilized Tribes, *Laws, Decisions, and Regulations Affecting the Work of the Commissioner to the Five Civilized Tribes, 1893 to 1906*(Washington, D.C.: Government Printing Office, 1906), 11–12. For the conflicting motives of supporters and opponents of severalty, see Loring Benson Priest, *Uncle Sam's Stepchildren: The Reformation of United States Indian Policy, 1865–1887* (New Brunswick: Rutgers University Press, 1942), 190–97; D. S. Otis, *The Dawes Act and the Allotment of Indian Lands*, ed. Francis Paul Prucha (Norman: University of Oklahoma Press, 1973), 18–32; Henry E. Fritz, *The Movement for Indian Assimilation* (Philadelphia: University of Pennsylvania Press, 1963),211–12.

60. Commissioner to the Five Civilized Tribes, *Laws, Decisions, and Regulations*, 12–13; Debo, *The Rise and Fall of the Choctaw Republic*, 248–60.

61. *Winton v. Amos* at 295.
62. Ibid., at 304–6; Angie Debo, *And Still the Waters Run: The Betrayal of the Five Civilized Tribes* (Princeton: Princeton University Press Paperbacks, 1972), 43.
63. Commission to the Five Civilized Tribes, *Report upon the Question "Whether the Mississippi Choctaws under Their Treaties Are Not Entitled to All the Rights of Choctaw Citizenship, Except an Interest in the Choctaw Annuities,"* January 28, 1898, Rights of the Mississippi Choctaw, 1898, vertical files—Choctaw Indians, Research Library, Oklahoma Historical Society, Oklahoma City; William O. Beall to the Commissioner of the Five Civilized Tribes, April 14, 1914, box 4, file 9, Patrick J. Hurley Collection, Western History Collections, University of Oklahoma Library, Norman.
64. *Jack Amos et al. v. The Choctaw Nation*, U.S. Court of the Central District of Indian Territory, No. 158 (1897), reprinted in Commissioner of Indian Affairs, *Report*, 55th Cong., 3d sess., September 26, 1898, H. Doc. 5, pp. 457–65; *Winton v. Amos* at 304–7.
65. *Winton v. Amos* at 290, 305–10; Debo, *And Still the Waters Run*, 43. Williams and his colleagues were responsible for inserting the following provision in the Indian Appropriation Act of June 7, 1897: "That the commission appointed to negotiate with the Five Civilized Tribes in the Indian Territory shall examine and report to Congress whether the Mississippi Choctaw under their treaties are not entitled to all the rights of Choctaw citizenship except an interest in the Choctaw annuities" (Kappler, *Indian Affairs*, 1:87).
66. Commissioner to the Five Civilized Tribes, *Laws, Decisions, and Regulations*, 20.
67. Commission to the Five Civilized Tribes, *Report as to Identification of Mississippi Choctaws*, 56th Cong., 1st sess., March 10, 1899, H. Doc. 5, p. 80.
68. Commissioner to the Five Civilized Tribes, *Laws, Decisions, and Regulations*, 65. Also see Secretary of the Interior Ethan A. Hitchcock to Commission to the Five Civilized Tribes, March 17, 1903, in *Five Civilized Tribes in Oklahoma* 62d Cong., 3d sess., March 4, 1913, S. Doc. 1139, pp. 37–39.
69. Kappler, *Indian Affairs*, 3:17; Commissioner of Indian Affairs, *Report*, 58th Cong., 2d sess., October 15, 1903, H. Doc. 5, p. 93; Commission to the Five Civilized Tribes, *Report for 1904*, 58th Cong., 3d sess., H. Doc. 5, pp. 14–15. For an essentially contemporaneous account of the pressures being applied to effect removal of the Choctaw, see John William Wade, "The Removal of the Mississippi Choctaws," *Publications of the Mississippi Historical Society* 8 (1904):397–426.
70. Kappler, *Indian Affairs*, 1:106. Later, in 1906, Congress enacted legislation (the so-called McCumber amendment) limiting the power of full-bloods to "alienate, sell, dispose of, or encumber in any manner any of the lands allotted to them for a period of twenty-five years . . . unless such restriction shall, prior to the expiration of said period, be removed by act of Congress" (ibid., 3:176–77). The results of the allotment policy in Indian Territory are detailed in Debo, *And Still the Waters Run*, and in Debo, *The Five Civilized Tribes of Oklahoma: Report on Social and Economic Conditions* (Philadelphia: Lyon and Armor for Indian Rights Association, 1951); Rennard Strickland, *The Indians in Oklahoma* (Norman: University of Oklahoma Press, 1980).
71. E. A. Hitchcock to Chief, Indian Territory Division, February 9, 1907, Samuel Adams to John H. Stephens, July 2, 1912, 62d Cong., 3d sess., S. Doc. 1139, 14–15, 34–36; Commission to the Five Civilized Tribes, *Report for 1907*, 60th Cong., 1st sess., H. Doc. 5, pp. 287–90; Commission to the Five Civilized Tribes, *Report for 1908*, 60th Cong., 2d sess., H. Doc. 1046, pp. 194–95; Debo, *And Still the Waters Run*, 47. There are several discrepancies in the sources cited above as to the number of persons enrolled. The number varies from 1,627 to 1,660. Some people identified as Mississippi Choctaw never moved to the West and were therefore not placed on the rolls.
72. Commission to the Five Civilized Tribes, *Report for 1907*, 60th Cong., 1st sess., H. Doc. 5, pp. 287–88; William S. Coker, "Pat Harrison's Efforts to Reopen the Choctaw

Citizenship Rolls," *Southern Quarterly* 3 (October 1964):39–60; Report of National Attorney for the Choctaw Nation to Commissioner Cato Sells, for the Quarter ending December 31, 1916, box 12, file 9, pp. 26–28, Hurley Collection.

73. This statement is based upon my reading of the *Congressional Record* for the period between the closing of the rolls in 1907 (60th Cong., 1st sess.) and the enactment of the final per capita payment to the western Choctaw in 1916 (64th Cong., 1st sess.). Also see Coker, "Pat Harrison's Efforts to Reopen the Choctaw Citizenship Rolls," 36–60; William F. Holmes, *The White Chief: James Kimble Vardaman* (Baton Rouge: Louisiana State University Press, 1970), 291; and note 77 below.

74. This statement is based upon my reading of the *Congressional Record* as cited in note 73 above. Also see Debo, *And Still the Waters Run*, 269–71. Oklahoma senator Robert L. Owen, who worked hard to prevent the reopening of the rolls, had earlier defended the rights of Mississippi Choctaw to citizenship in the Choctaw Nation without having to remove to Indian Territory. See *Winton v. Amos* at 284–342. During the congressional hearings on the claims of the Mississippi Choctaw in 1914, Choctaw attorney Patrick Hurley accused Harry J. Cantwell, an attorney for Mississippi Choctaw claimants, of "besmirching the character" of Senator Owen to "divert attention from his own questionable transactions" when Cantwell referred to Owen's efforts to enroll "absentee" Choctaw; see *House Hearings on Enrollment*, 370–71, 480. For other examples of the charges and countercharges made by both sides, see *Congressional Record*, 63d Cong., 2d sess., 10719–23, 11736, and note 77 below.

75. Choctaw council quoted in Coker, "Pat Harrison's Efforts to Reopen the Choctaw Citizenship Rolls," 40.

76. The quotations are from *House Hearings on Enrollment*, 532. The 1913 memorial of the Choctaw and Chickasaw nations cited in note 52 was drafted by Hurley. For additional information on Hurley's efforts to protect the Choctaw Nation from bogus "absentee" Choctaw claimants, see Debo, *And Still the Waters Run*, 269–70; Russell D. Buhite, *Patrick J. Hurley and American Foreign Policy* (Ithaca: Cornell University Press, 1973),19–22; Parker La Moore, *"Pat" Hurley: The Story of an American* (New York: Brewer, Warren and Putnam, 1932), 70–73; Don Lohbeck, *Patrick J. Hurley* (Chicago: Regnery, 1956), 50–55.

77. Kappler, *Indian Affairs*, 4:76–77; Report of National Attorney for the Choctaw Nation to Commissioner Cato Sells, for the Quarter ending December 31, 1916, box 12, file 9, pp. 10–11, Hurley Collection. In March 1916, before the passage of the per capita payment, Mississippian John Williams, then a U.S. senator, lambasted the Oklahoma delegation for thwarting his efforts on behalf of the Mississippi Choctaw. Williams stated: "I have stood here two Congresses, and I have stood in the House—I do not remember how many Congresses—and I have defeated Indian Affairs Committee after Indian Affairs Committee with a vote of one house or the other. I have defeated the Indian Affairs Committee of this House—the Senate—twice, and once when I was sick in bed and could not come here the Senate, by procrastination and filibustering, carried over the Indian appropriation bill, under the guidance and leadership of my colleague, until the Indian appropriation bill itself was defeated, rather than leave these people without their rights under the law; and the Indian Affairs Committee in this appropriation bill, under the dominancy of the State of Oklahoma, has paid no more attention to the views of the Senate than if the Senate of the United States had not existed" (*Congressional Record*, 64th Cong., 1st sess., 4923). It should be noted, however, that the 1916 legislation included funds to enable the secretary of the interior to investigate the condition of the Mississippi Choctaw and to report to Congress on their need for the land and school facilities; see Kappler, *Indian Affairs* 4:68.

78. *House Hearings on Condition of the Mississippi Choctaws*, 117. For examples of Venable's earlier activities on behalf of the Choctaw, see *Congressional Record*, 64th Cong., 1st sess., 228–29; 65th Cong., 3d sess., 1136–40.

79. *House Hearing on Condition of the Mississippi Choctaws*, 117–72. For the quotations, see 137, 147.

80. *Congressional Record*, 65th Cong., 2d sess., 5113; Kappler, *Indian Affairs*, 4:158; Commissioner of Indian Affairs, *Report for 1918* (Washington, D.C.: Government Printing Office, 1918), 83–84 (quotations); Peterson, "The Mississippi Band of Choctaw Indians," 110–11.

81. Mississippi Band of Choctaw Indians Tribal Council, *Chahta Hapia Hoke: We Are Choctaw* (Philadelphia, Miss., 1981), 14.

82. *U.S. Federal Register* 9:14907–8; Mississippi Band of Choctaw Indians, *Constitution and By-Laws of the Mississippi Band of Choctaw Indians, Ratified April 20, 1945* (Washington, D.C.: Government Printing Office, 1946), 1–4.

83. See *United States v. John*, 98 Supreme Court 2541 (1978).

84. For the official tribal history of the Mississippi Band of Choctaw Indians that discusses the events leading to the current era of self-determination, see Mississippi Band of Choctaw Indians, *Chahta Hapia Hoke*.

2

Choctaw Farmsteads in Mississippi, 1830

Rufus Ward

The Choctaw Indians in Mississippi in the 1830s lived in a fashion little different from that of the white settlers moving into the new state. Research that has focused on the small farms of the Choctaw in Lowndes, Clay, and Oktibbeha counties in Mississippi has provided documentary and artifactual evidence dating to the time of the Treaty of Dancing Rabbit Creek. During this period the Choctaw lived in log or frame houses, raised livestock, farmed, used English-made dishes, and often enjoyed economic status that was equal to, if not higher than, that of the early white settlers in the area. The Choctaw who were forced off their land during the early 1830s were a civilized people.

The Treaty of Dancing Rabbit Creek, which was signed in 1830, mandated the final removal of the Choctaw Indian Nation from Mississippi. The treaty allowed Choctaw families, however, to remain in Mississippi if they had a dwelling and at least two acres of land under cultivation.[1] Courthouse records indicate the number of acres that families managed in 1830, and artifacts collected from some of the reservation sites furnish additional clues to the life of the Mississippi Choctaw in 1830.

The reservation sites that I will discuss in this chapter are located in Oktibbeha, Clay, and Lowndes counties, Mississippi, and represent the Choctaw living in the Northeastern district of the Choctaw Nation during the 1830s. Although the sites are scattered, they seem to be grouped together in loose clusters or communities connected by roads and paths. Several clusters appear along Tibbee Creek, the boundary line between the Choctaw and Chickasaw nations. Another cluster, including approximately eighteen families, centered around Oktoc, in southeastern Oktibbeha County. The reservation sites were no doubt farmsteads, comprising a dwelling house and from 2 to 200 acres of cultivated land. The cultivated land—most likely including a cornfield—was usually located on a creek bottom, with enclosures such as cowpens on terraces adjacent to the creek bottom.[2] The house typically occupied the first terrace. The personal property inventory of Tisha Homa indicates some of the farming implements that the Choctaw used on these farmsteads. Tisha Homa, called a "Choctaw Captain" in his estate file, died in Lowndes County in 1836. He owned two axes, two hoes, a hatchet, a hammer, a bell collar, a bridle, and a plow in addition to four horses, a yearling, and a colt.[3] The poorer Choctaw lived in log cabins and, the wealthier ones—captains or chiefs—in wood frame houses. Cushman described the log cabins as being comfortable two-room houses similar to those of many of the white settlers.[4] Although no known Choctaw structures still stand in any of the three counties under consideration, a description of the Choctaw Council House, which was located on the Noxubee River in southern Oktibbeha County, has been recorded. It was built of split poplar logs and measured about twenty feet by thirty feet in length, with gable ends east and west and a door on the north.[5] Moshulitubbee, an important chief of the Northeast district, constructed a frame house in Noxubee County in 1819 with two stories, two rooms on each floor, and a porch across the front. Furnishings were usually sparse—a table and chairs but no beds. Even in Moshulitubbee's house, individuals slept on pallets.[6] In Tisha Homa's inventory, the only furnishings listed are a table and two chairs. Surface collections from five reservation sites include artifacts associated with the Choctaw who lived on those sites. These artifacts shed some light on the effect that the white culture had exerted on the Choctaw in Mississippi by the 1830s. The most common artifacts found were ceramic fragments of pottery made by the Choctaw and manufactured earthenwares principally from England. On some sites the percentage of English-made earthenware fragments is greater, while on other sites the percentage of Chickachae combed, finely made Choctaw ware is greater. The percentage of utilitarian ware made by the Choctaw is about the same on the sites. The increase in the use of

Choctaw Farmsteads, 1830

A brass thimble and blue transfer-printed whiteware, collected on the Hotana Reservation northern site, and a brass armband or gorget, collected on the Yokatubbee Reservation site. *Courtesy of Rufus Ward*

English ceramics appears to have caused a decrease in the manufacture of the Choctaw ceramics of better quality, although collections were made from a limited number of sites, and it is therefore not possible to determine that such was the case throughout the Choctaw Nation. Items of personal adornment have also been found on the sites—manufactured ornaments in the form of glass beads, a metal gorget, and a brass thimble without a tip. Ornaments of Choctaw manufacture (disc- and barrel-shaped shell beads) were found on only one of the sites. As with finely made Choctaw pottery, mass-produced ornaments seem slowly to have replaced the native ones.

While several gunflints have been found, only three arrow points which could be dated to the period have come from the Choctaw sites. Tisha Homa's inventory included a shotgun, further indicating that firearms were replacing the bow and arrow as a primary weapon. Tisha Homa's inventory also included iron knives and tools, explaining the absence of stone tools from any of the site collections. Eating utensils changed with the advent of Europeans too. Late in the 1820s, a visitor to Moshulitubbee's house described a meal during which everyone ate with wooden spoons from a single dish.[7] This traditional method of serving food did not last much longer. English ceramic fragments indicate that cups, saucers, dinner plates, and pitchers were used, and a silver spoon was found on one of the smaller farmsteads. The inventory of Tisha Homa lists two brass kettles, two pots, an oven, nine plates, a pitcher, a tin pan, a water bucket, and a broken set of knives and forks.[8] The Choctaw in Mississippi in 1830 had reached a degree of cultural sophistication and affluence not often apparent from popular histories.

In an 1886 article in the *North American Review*, Jefferson Davis described them as receptive to "civilization" and as having homes, cattle, crops, schools, and their own laws.[9] George Miller has delineated four levels of social and economic status as reflected by early nineteenth-century earthenwares.[10] Although all four levels are present in the ceramics found on the Choctaw sites, the fourth level, transfer-printed designs—the most expensive earthenware ceramics on

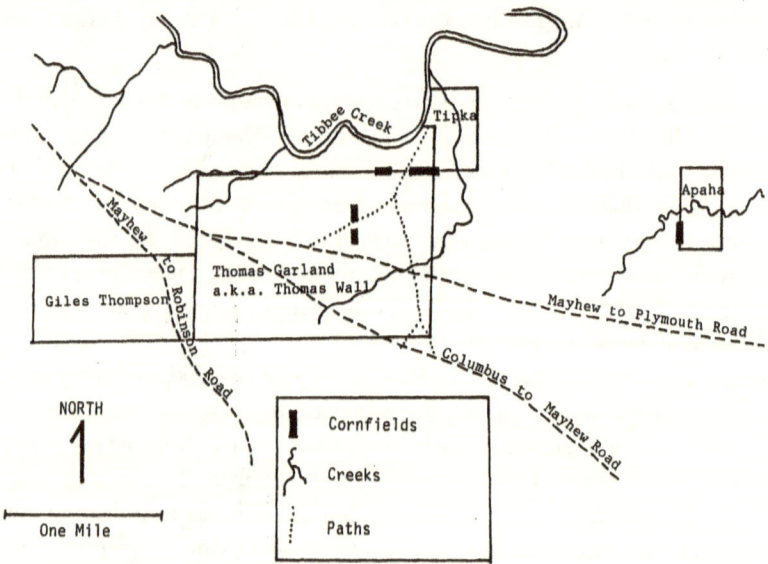

The farmsteads of Giles Thompson, Thomas Wall, Tipka, and Apaha were reserved under the Treaty of Dancing Rabbit Creek. The cornfields, roads, and paths have been added according to information contained in 1833 survey notes. *Courtesy of Rufus Ward*

Choctaw Farmsteads, 1830

the market at the time—is significantly in evidence. These ceramics are comparable to those used by many of the white settlers in the area. As late as 1830, half of all the houses in Columbus, which had a population of almost 700, were log dwellings. Several prominent white settlers even purchased Choctaw houses and moved into them.[11] The evidence available in Clay, Oktibbeha, and Lowndes counties suggests that the economic status of many of the Choctaw during the early 1830s was commensurate with that of the whites in the same period.

Thomas Wall, also known as Thomas Garland, signed the Treaty of Dancing Rabbit Creek as an individual who was entitled to a section and a half of land. The tract included his place of residence in 1830 and any improvements he had made to the land. Wall was granted all of section 8 and the west half of section 9, township 19, range 16 east, near what is now Clay County, Mississippi. The original U.S. Survey field notes from 1832 locate four Indian cornfields and three paths on this reservation. The notes also show where the Columbus-to-Mayhew and Mayhew-to-Plymouth roads crossed the site. Surface collections contain some mid-nineteenth-century historic material, but nothing that is definitely of Choctaw derivation.

Siles Bohanon's reservation was located in township 21, range 13 east. In 1832, he sold all 79.9 acres, "land and premises," to Howell Peedon for $100. The deed indicates that Bohanon had received the land initially because he had cultivated seven acres of land in 1830.[12] On a ridge next to a creek bottom about 100 yards north of the reservation's southern boundary line, surface collections yielded fragments of an early nineteenth-century gunflint; earthenware with blue embossed edges, circa early 1820s to early 1840s; blue monochrome whiteware, circa 1830–1845; and undecorated whiteware. These artifacts indicate that the site was probably occupied during the early nineteenth century. Moreover, an elderly resident of the area recalled that between 1910 and 1915 she had visited a dogtrot house near the spot where the artifacts were found. She remembered that the northern end of the house had been constructed around what she believed to have been an old single-pen log house, the earliest style of house constructed in the area.[13]

The Hotana Reservation, consisting of 82.88 acres, was located in township 18, range 16 east, in Lowndes County. U.S. Survey field notes

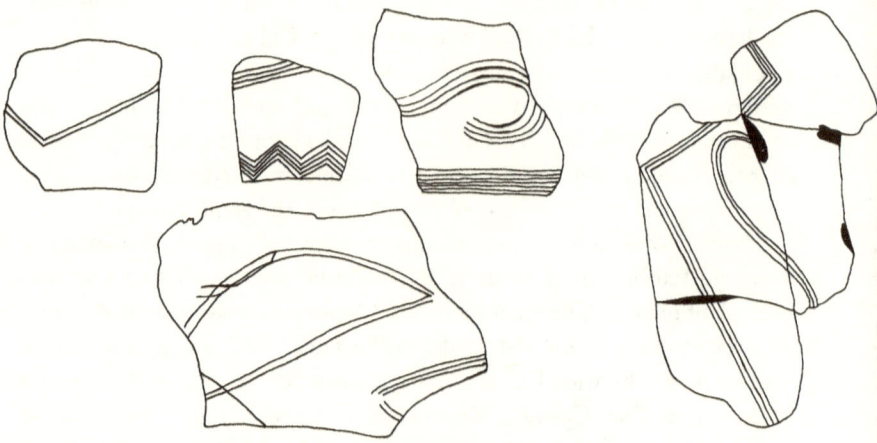

Chickachae combed ceramics collected at the Hotana Reservation northern site. *Courtesy of Rufus Ward*

and map show a road from the Mayhew Mission to the Robinson Road, passing through the reservation. The map also shows a large field about one mile southeast of the reservation, and the notes mention another field one mile south of the reservation. The site is presently cultivated as a soybean field. Surface collections reveal both Choctaw and early nineteenth-century European artifacts indicating Choctaw occupation: Chickachae combed pottery; European trade beads; creamware ceramics; black and blue transfer-printed whitewares, circa 1830–1870; and a broken bottle neck, circa 1820–1830.[14] A brass thimble and a wrought nail were also found at this site. In the southeast corner of the reservation, surface collections produced Chickachae combed pottery, transfer-printed whitewares, shell-edged decorated whitewares, sprigware whiteware and pearlware and slip-banded whiteware, a silver teaspoon, and a faceted blue glass bead.[15] The Yokatubbee site, a reservation of 82.88 acres, adjoined the Hotana site and was located in township 19, range 16 east in Lowndes County. The Mayhew Mission–Robinson Road ran about 200 yards west, and a field was located about three-quarters of a mile southeast of the site, which is also presently cultivated as a soybean field. Surface collections made on the southwest corner of the reservation included Chickachae combed ceramic

Choctaw Farmsteads, 1830

and shell-tempered native ceramic fragments; a madison point of white chert; and artifacts of European manufacture. The latter included fragments of blue monochrome pearlware, circa 1815–1835; transfer-printed whiteware, circa 1830–1870; green sprigware whiteware, circa 1830–1845; blue shell-edged decorated ware with a bud motif, circa 1820–1840's; and decorated pearl whitewares with blue-embossed edges, circa early 1820s to early 1840s.[16]

Transfer-printed whiteware shards in several different colors have also been found on the site, including one shard which appears to be a fragment of a bowl with a pattern showing General Lafayette landing at Castle Garden, New York. The pattern was made by Clews in

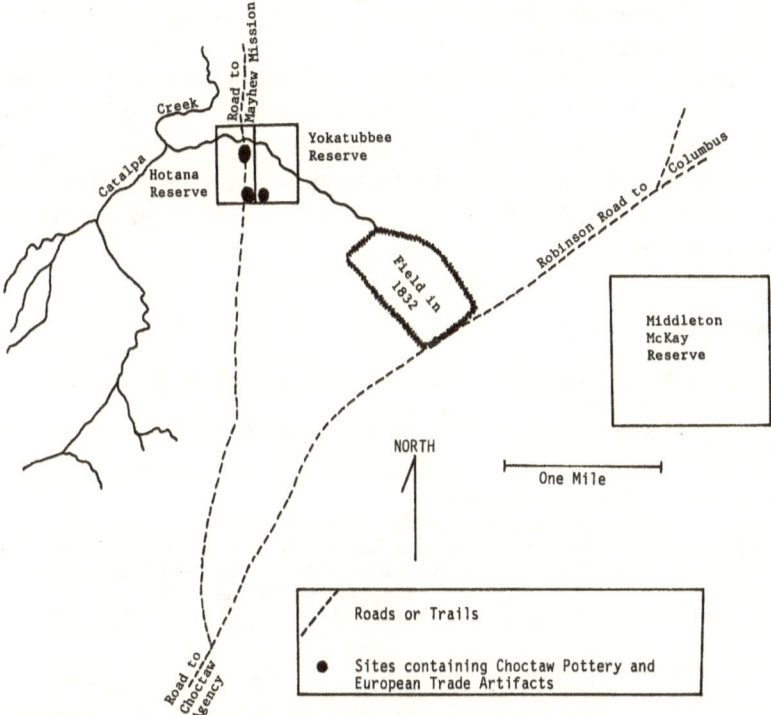

The Yokatubbee, Hotana, and Middleton McKay reservations, drawn using data from U.S. government field notes, from the original U.S. survey, from deed records, and from sites located by surface collecting of artifacts. *Courtesy of Rufus Ward*

England, circa 1825.[17] A maker's mark on one shard is identifiable as Enoch Wood and Sons of England, a firm which operated between 1818 and 1846.[18] Other objects found on the site include brown and olive-colored glass bottle fragments typical of the glass bottles used during the first quarter of the nineteenth century and metal artifacts—wrought nails, cut nails with applied heads, and a metal band which is punched at one end and may have been used as a gorget.[19]

The artifacts found on the Yokatubbee Reservation indicate the site was occupied between the early 1820s and the early 1830s. Deed records show that the reservation had been occupied by 1830 but that the Choctaw occupation ended in 1832.[20] Several of the decorations on the English ceramics on the site occur also in collections from other Choctaw sites and from white sites near Columbus that were occupied at the same time period.

The courthouse records and artifacts from the farmsteads of the 1830s show that the Choctaw who attempted to remain in Mississippi after the signing of the Treaty of Dancing Rabbit Creek enjoyed a life-style that was comparable to, and often better than, that of the white settlers who were moving into the newly opened land that had once been the Choctaw Nation.

Notes

1. *The Revised Code of the Statute Laws of the State of Mississippi* (Jackson: E. Barksdale, 1857), 706–14.
2. Clay County, Land Record Books (on file in the Chancery Clerk's office in the Clay County Court House, West Point, Miss.).
3. Lowndes County, Chancery Court, Cause No. 135, *Estate of Tisha Homa, otherwise called Captain Red Pepper*, 1836.
4. Horatio B. Cushman, *History of the Choctaw, Chickasaw, and Natchez Indians* (1899; reprint, New York: Russell and Russell, 1972), 173.
5. H. S. Halbert, "The Last Indian Council on the Noxubee River," *Publications of the Mississippi Historical Society* 4 (1901):276 (hereafter cited as PMHS).
6. H. S. Halbert, "Origin of Mashulaville," PMHS 7 (1903):389.
7. Ibid.
8. *Estate of Tisha Homa*, Cause No. 135.
9. Anna Grace Love, unpublished manuscript, 1960, in author's possession.
10. George L. Miller, "Classification and Economic Scaling of Nineteenth Century Ceramics," *Historical Archaeology* 14 (1980): 1–40.
11. W. L. Lipscomb, *A History of Columbus, Mississippi* (Birmingham, Ala.: Press of Dispatch Printing, 1909), 62.
12. Clay County, Land Record Books, Book F, 5.
13. Sam O. Brookes, Mississippi Department of Archives and History, personal com-

munication, 1980; George L. Miller, National Historic Parks and Sites Branch, Ottawa, Ontario, Canada, personal communication, 1980; W. Lee Minnerly, Michigan State University, personal communication, 1980; Mrs. Marlin W. Carty, personal communication, 1980; Eugene M. Wilson, *Alabama Folk Houses* (Montgomery: Alabama Historical Commission, 1975), 25.

14. Richard A. Marshall, "An Example of Chickachae Combed Pottery," *Mississippi Archaeology* 13, no. 1 (1978): 23;George Irvin Quimby, *Indian Culture and European Trade Goods* (Madison: University of Wisconsin Press, 1966), 85–90; Ivor Noel Hume, *A Guide to Artifacts of Colonial America* (New York: Knopf, 1976), 129–31; Minnerly, personal communication, 1980; Robert Sonderman, Michigan State University, personal communication, 1980; Rufus A. Ward, Jr., "English Earthenwares Associated with Early Nineteenth Century Choctaw Sites," *Mississippi Archaeology* 18, no. 1 (1983): 37.

15. Ivor Noel Hume, *Guide to Artifacts*, 129–31.

16. Minnerly, personal communication, 1980; ibid.; Miller, personal communication, 1980; ibid.; Ward, "English Earthenwares," 39.

17. N. Hudson Moore, *The Old China Book* (New York: Tudor Publishing Co., 1937), 29.

18. Geoffrey Godden, *Encyclopaedia of British Pottery and Porcelain Marks* (New York: Bonanza, 1964), 686.

19. Ward, "English Earthenwares," 38.

20. Ibid.

3

The Role of Mixed-Bloods in Mississippi Choctaw History

Samuel J. Wells

The thousands of mixed-bloods among the Choctaw Indians prior to removal played important roles as intermediaries between the tribe and American officials on the frontier. Identification of them is necessary if we are to see their influence on the outcome of American history in proper perspective. First, however, we must lay aside the illusion that frontier history was a mere "cowboy and Indian" conflict in which the noble brave clashed with the greedy land grabber, or the dirty savage molested the innocent homesteader. The presence of English-speaking mixed-bloods and Choctaw-speaking white men throughout most of the postcontact period suggests that frontier confrontations were significantly more complex.[1] The mixed-bloods and their white parents, called countrymen because they lived in Indian country, were both the buffer against and the catalyst for white intrusions upon Indian lands and customs.

The role of mixed-bloods in Choctaw history has been little investigated beyond the identification of a few of the more prominent removal and postremoval leaders in the group (table 1). The classic Indian histories written by Angie Debo, Robert Cotterill, and Francis Paul Prucha make only few references to these people,[2] and Arthur De Rosier, Jr., W. David Baird, Arrell Gibson, and the venerable Choctaw historian Horatio Cushman discuss the mixed-bloods at only somewhat greater length.[3]

According to historian Thomas P. Abernethy, the mixed-bloods and countrymen along the Tombigbee River valley, which runs from the

Table 1.
Notable Mixed-Bloods

John Adcock	William Hollinger
Susan Anoba	Calvert Howell
James Bailey	Adam James
Betsey Beams	George Johnston
Silas Bohannon	William Jones
John Bond	Arthur Kearney
Zadoc Brashear	Greenwood Leflore
Allen Carney	Anne Lewellyn
John Cravat	William Lightfoot
Charles Durant	John McGillivray
Michael Elliot	Joel Nail
Josiah Fletcher	Betsey Pinson
David Folsom	Peter Ptichlynn
William Foster	John Randon
James Gardner	Samuel Sealy
William Hall	George Stiggins
Robert Hancock	Arthur Turnbull
George Harkins	Tandy Walker
Daniel Harris	Billy Wright
John Hinson	

Source: Compiled by the Author

Tennessee border southward to the Gulf, "had filtered through the Indian country from the time of the Revolution onward" and were "Tory refugees . . . , patriots . . . , and traders with the Indians. The blood of these men was various: English and Scotish traders mingled with Yankee frontiersmen, and many of them had taken native wives. . . . These half-breeds were often men of wealth, and no distinction of race seems to have been made in the rugged life of the frontier."[4]

Interestingly, the derogatory names such as "half-breed" and "squaw-man" that are frequently found in western literature and movies are less evident in the records of the Old Southwest. Many mixed-bloods were able to live in either Indian or white society.[5] The critical factor affecting their ability to choose between the two lifestyles was less the amount of "blood" that they had inherited than the kind of "culture" they displayed. This manifestation of culture is crucial in understanding the role played by the early sons and daughters of white men who lived in Indian country; the degree to which someone acted either Indian or white determined his treatment by his contemporaries more than the quantity of Indian blood in his veins. In reality the question of blood is a false one, not only because it is extremely difficult to measure, but also because the father of a mixed-blood child cannot be conclusively identified. Lineage traced through the mother's side, as was customary among the Choctaw Indians, is more accurate than the patrilineality of Euro-Americans, although we must search mainly patrilineal records in order to trace the mixed-bloods.

Problems are associated with the term "mixed-blood," which implies the measurement of "blood" as a determinant of race. This problem has long bothered scholars, and some have suggested the substitution of "mestizo". but since "mestizo" has for centuries been used in connection with Latin American mixed-bloods, it could be misleading in the present context. Actually, "mixed blood" is a relatively mild and neutral term and is relatively less confusing than "ambicultural" or "bicultural."[6] The term "mixed-blood" appears often in official records such as Indian censuses and nineteenth-century correspondence. Oddly enough, the Bureau of Indian Affairs still uses a blood quantum test to determine the legal degree of a person's "Indianness."

Even from the time of DeSoto, the mixed-bloods and countrymen figured prominently as shapers of events. A shipwrecked Spaniard held captive by Indians, having learned his captor's language, acted as interpreter when DeSoto first landed in Florida in 1539. This man's ability to interpret for both sides made it possible for the conquistador to take hostages and find bearers for captured Spanish supplies.[7] Without a bilingual go-between, DeSoto might have been unable to ravage southeastern lands.

Other white countrymen entered Indian lands at an ever-increasing rate after 1700, when Spain and France sought to counter the British influence with Indians through the use of trade goods. English colonists offered the Indians manufactured articles in trade for deerskins and other peltry. An especially large number of Scotch and Scotch-Irish tradesmen eagerly undertook to live and trade in Indian country. The French also had "coureurs de bois," who made homes among the tribes of the Mississippi Valley, took Indian wives, and raised families just as readily as their Celtic cousins.

Not until the late 1700s, however, did the countrymen and their mixed-blood offspring begin to influence the fate of the southeastern Indians. The Choctaw received a large number of white and mixed-blood Tories who, not wanting to join in the revolt against England, fled from their homes in the colonies and sought refuge in Indian country.[8] The war also brought the Spanish back into the coastal areas of present-day Mississippi, Alabama, and Florida—a region from which they had been forced by the British at the end of the French and Indian War in 1763.

The earlier confrontation between England and the French-Spanish forces constitutes a landmark in Indian history. Not only was France temporarily evicted from the North American continent after the war, but Spain also lost its Florida possessions east of the Mississippi River. The realignment of power left the French-loving Choctaw obliged to contend with their former English enemies as the predominant European power in the area.[9] In a short time several Choctaw treaties with the new British government ceded land in the Natchez district and among the Alabama-Tombigbee settlements north of Mobile.[10]

The English immediately began consolidating their newly acquired territories, but before two decades had passed, the insurrection in the American colonies gave Spain the chance to recoup its former Gulf possessions. Thus the last years of the American revolution witnessed the return of Spanish-sponsored traders and agents among the various Indian tribes. The Choctaw in particular were courted by the Spanish contingents at Mobile and Natchez, and new countrymen began appearing among the piney woods of the Tombigbee valley.[11]

Because the Choctaw had long enjoyed a position of trading leadership among southeastern tribes, they were attractive to European commercial enterprises seeking furs and skins.[12] The Spanish government, in keeping with its borderlands policy of erecting buffer territories around the gold supply, sought to placate both the Indians and the mainly white British merchants by allowing trade between the two. Tribes happily supplied with tools and textiles were less of a concern to the Spanish. The Iberian governors followed a similar policy with the neighboring Creeks and Chickasaw, placing a barrier of friendly Indians between themselves and the boisterous Americans in the southern colonies and along the Ohio Valley.

Also present in Indian country throughout this period were European military contingents based along the Gulf Coast, especially in Mobile, New Orleans, and Pensacola. Although these soldiers were not as important a presence as their mercantile-minded brethren, they exercised some influence among the tribes and sired some offspring of mixed blood, mainly after retiring from the military to settle on land grants near Indian country.[13]

Together these Tories, tradesmen, and soldiers contributed to a new generation of mixed-bloods which assimilated the New World and the Old World, making possible the eventual erosion of Indian culture. The matrilineal nature of southeastern Indian tribes offered the offspring of white countrymen an extremely effective way of attaining leadership positions. Their children, endowed with the white father's language and European "business sense," also automatically enjoyed the mother's clan status and tribal affiliations.[14] Is it any wonder that these sons of countrymen rose rapidly in their roles as interpreters, intermediaries and entrepreneurs? For they enjoyed the confidence and kinship of both races.

The earliest recorded white settlers in Choctaw country included the Cravats, Durants, LaFleurs, and Perrys as well as the Juzans and Nails.[15] Homesteading along the Tombigbee tributaries and the increasingly traveled Natchez-to-Nashville trail in the late 1700s, these frontiersmen almost without exception married Choctaw and Chickasaw women and cleared plantation lands in the very heart of the Indian nations. By the beginning of the nineteenth century, the countrymen and their offspring were tending huge herds of black-faced cattle, were shipping bales of cotton downriver to Spanish Mobile, and were establising themselves as innkeepers and ferrymen along the early frontier roads and horsepaths. Their lives on the early American frontier were fascinating.[16]

The LaFleur family patriarchs, Louis and Michael, emigrated from Canada after the British defeat of France in 1763 and settled along the upper Pearl River in present-day Neshoba County, Mississippi. Louis married the mixed-blood daughters of John Cravat and sired a large family. His son Greenwood eventually became chief of all the Choctaw nation. Greenwood later amassed a fortune from cotton plantations in the Delta region of Mississippi and joined the elite ranks of the planter class as a member of the state legislature. He attained unusual economic success in the antebellum south.[17]

John Cravat also came from a French family and married into both the Choctaw and Chickasaw nations. Horatio Cushman credits Louis Durant, another Frenchman, with the introduction of cattle into the western Choctaw Nation in 1770.[18] Durant drove herds upcountry from Mobile and allowed them to range freely on Pearl River canebrakes and grasslands.

Pierre Juzan, still another Frenchman, acted as a commissary, or trader, for the Spanish after their reoccupation of Mobile in the waning days of the American Revolution and raised a family in the Six Towns district, near the headwaters of the Chickasawhay River. The Juzans, like the LaFleurs, would produce chiefs to lead the Choctaw Nation during the removal period.[19]

Celts and Anglo-Saxons also contributed chiefs to the nation, being particularly represented by the Pitchlynns and the Folsoms. David Folsom, the son of Carolinian Nathaniel Folsom and Aiahnichih Ohoyoh of the Choctaw Nation, figured prominently in the intertribal political clashes preceding removal. He became the chief of the southern towns and also a leading frontier preacher. He married the mixed-blood Rhoda Nail. People of mixed blood often married, subsequently forming a social circle apart from that of their pure-blood Indian relatives. The white man's religion, science, and culture thus took root in the Indian nation.[20]

No Choctaw of mixed blood enjoyed the respect of both the white and red nations more than Peter Pitchlynn. His British father, John Pitchlynn, played a very active role in Choctaw history, acting as interpreter at the signing of the Treaty of Hopewell with the United States in 1786 until his death shortly after the commencement of removal in the 1830s. Peter did not really rise to leadership until the preremoval period of political upheaval in the tribe. He, like his father, was a staunch supporter of the U.S. government and advised it about the presence and influence of anti-American foreigners in the nation.[21] His mother was Sophia Folsom, and his wife, Rhoda Folsom; most of the mixed-bloods were related to each other within only a couple of generations.[22] Furthermore, it seems to have been customary for countrymen to marry Indian sisters, either two simultaneously or taking the spouse's sister as a second wife if the first died.

Some apparently white countrymen were really Indian mixed-bloods who came from the East. Once they had settled in Indian country, they wrote their mixed-blood friends and relatives in Carolina and Georgia, inviting them to come share the comforts of Choctaw country.[23] How many of the new arrivals were kith and kin is not fully known, and the many family histories now being collected by regional genealogists will doubtless prove invaluable to historians.

The Indian connection is sometimes denied or overlooked by genealogists who are not committed to accuracy, of course, but existing evidence is sufficient to link many prominent southern families with an Indian heritage. Many frontier towns and settlements of the Old Southwest received their names from the original settlers, and in many cases these settlers prove to have mixed-bloods. The Mississippi towns of Colbert, Durant, Greenwood, and Turnbull represent only a few such places.[24]

Perhaps the best way to comprehend the influence of mixed-bloods is to compare their size as a group to that of the Choctaw tribe at the time of removal. Most estimates place the tribal population at 20,000–25,000 people during the eighteenth century. If the average household included five persons, there were 4,000–5,000 households. The mixed-blood population consisted of at least 1,000 households, or roughly 20 percent of the tribe. In other words, the mixed bloods composed a very large segment and one which exercised growing control over tribal decisions.[25]

The large number of Anglo-Saxon and Celtic names appearing on treaties also indicates the influence of mixed-bloods. The Treaty of Dancing Rabbit Creek, for example, contained 170 tribal signatures.[26] Of this total, 126 Indian names appear, leaving 44 non-Indian names (table 2), or 74 percent Indian names and 26 percent names of other provenance. Most of the nontraditional names probably belonged to mixed-bloods.

I have collected thousands of names from records such as eighteenth- and nineteenth-century Spanish census records; *American State Papers* (both *Land Claims* and *Indian Affairs*); the Armstrong removal census roll; government corespondence before, during, and after removal; the writings of nineteenth-century regional historians; and records of the various Indian commissions that investigated Choctaw land claims throughout the nineteenth century. After computer sorting and collation, there remained more than a thousand mixed-blood names of heads of households. In most cases the identification is substantiated by several sources.[27]

Observers in Choctaw country during the preremoval debates in Washington, D.C., informed the government that various white men living in Choctaw country were actively couonseling the tribe to reject removal. With perhaps conscious irony, the mixed-blood David Folsom wrote the Choctaw agent: "We are sorry to hear that the Secretary of War has the impression, that the white men who reside among us, pervert our minds so that we are unwilling to remove toward the land of the West . . . None of the White men who are with us, have the direction of us; we are simply a nation of red men."[28]

The fact that Folsom, a mixed-blood frontier preacher and elected regional chief, could count himself a red man and could speak for the tribe suggests the degree to which mixed-bloods were able to exercise control just before removal. In 1826 an American delegation seeking further cessions of Choctaw land interpreted the situation differently:

Table 2.
Mixed-Blood Signers of the Treaty of Dancing Rabbit Creek

Zadoc Brashears	Greenwood Leflore
Jerry Carney	Thomas Leflore
Robert Cole	Daniel McCurtain
Silas D. Fisher	James McKing
James Fletcher	John McKolbery
David Folsom	Joel H. Nail
Isaac Folsom	Eden Nelson
Jacob Folsom	Levi Perkins
Robert Folsom	Isaac Perry
Hugh A. Foster	Lewis Perry
Thomas W. Foster	Jno. Pitchlynn, Jr.
William Foster	P. P. Pitchlynn
John Garland	Silas D. Pitchlynn
Benjm. James	James Shield
Isaac James	William Trahorn
Charles Jones	James Vaughn
Isaac Jones	William Wade
John Jones	John Waide
Pierre Juzan	Thomas Wall
James Karnes	John Washington
Joseph Kincaide	Lewis Wilson
Hiram King	Sam S. Worcester

Source: Kappler, *Indian Affairs: Laws and Treaties* (1904), vol. 2, 315–17.

"The government seems to be in the hands principally of half-breeds and white men, who dictate to some of them, without regard to the interest of the poor Indians."[29]

James McDonald, the son of a countryman, was sent to Washington as a youth to live with and work for the secretary of Indian trade, Thomas Loraine McKenny. The child's obvious intelligence and quick mind won him special attention from government officials. McDonald succeeded at his studies, eventually passed the bar, and returned to the new state of Mississippi. He later acted as spokesperson of the 1824 Choctaw delegation to Washington, D.C. (three of the seven delegates were mixed-bloods) and smoothly negotiated a treaty with Secretary of War Calhoun and Secretary of Indian Affairs McKenny. He also wrote an eloquent oration against removal delivered before the Congress of the United States during that time. McDonald eventually received land reservations from the Treaty of Dancing Rabbit Creek in 1830, but he died, a broken man, before he had received his land.[30]

Although not all mixed-bloods held leadership positions, most of them owned improved farmland which they sought to protect during treaty talks (table 3). It remains to be determined whether or not the mixed-bloods obtained land at the expense of the full-blood Choctaw. Most of the recipients of land reservations may have been mixed-bloods, and possibly most of the Indians removed in the 1830s were full-bloods or mixed-bloods who embraced an Indian life-style.

After removal several groups of mixed-bloods remained behind in the Mississippi Black Belt region and in the Delta on their cotton plantations, continued to expand their already large slave holdings, and generally lived the lives of southern gentlemen. A large number of agrarian, slave-holding mixed bloods also migrated westward with the bulk of the tribe and formed a powerful nucleus for the civic growth and "civilization" of the Oklahoma Choctaw.[31] Conversely, full-bloods and mixed-bloods who embraced traditional Choctaw ways stayed behind in Mississippi, some roaming the land, others sharecropping and eventually blending in with free blacks or poor whites.

There is ample evidence that more than a few "first families of Mississippi," whose forebears settled in the state during revolutionary and territorial times, had mixed-blood ancestors. Many other ancestors were actually countrymen who crossed and recrossed both social and

Table 3.
Recipients of Land Named in the Treaty of Dancing Rabbit Creek

Turner Brashears	Michael Leflore
Vaughn Brashears	Tobias Leflore
John Bond	William Leflore
James Campbell	Samuel Long
Susan (James) Colbert	Middleton Mackey
Jo Doke	T. Magaha
L. Durans	D. McCurtain
Thos. Everge	James McDonald
Polly Fillecuthey	Alexander McKee
Silas Fisher	Joel H. Nail
Moses Foster	Molly Nail
S. Foster	Robert Nail
Israel Folsom	G. Nelson
Jacob Folsom	Jack Pitchlynn
Samuel Garland	John Pitchlynn
Thomas Garland	Peter Pitchlynn
James D. Hamilton	Thomas Pitchlynn
G. W. Harkins	Silas Pitchlynn
Willis Harkins	Charles Scott
R. Harris	Giles Thompson
P. Hays	Peggy Trahern
George Hunter	Wesley Train
Benjamin James	William Train
Robert Jones	J. Vaughn
Pierre Juzan	D. W. Wall
William Juzan	Noah Wall
Benjamin Leflore	Samuel Worcester
Louis Leflore	Allen Yates

Source: Kappler, Indian Affairs: Laws and Treaties (1904), vol. 2, 317–8.

political boundaries with ease. The two seminal social groups left a cultural legacy of enormous proportions.

Today several thousand recognized full-blood Choctaw live in Mississippi, and several multiracial isolated groups claim Choctaw lineage. Most early mixed-blood families, however, simply accepted roles in the white communities that sprang up around them. Their survivors are today a large proportion of the modern population. The experience of the Choctaw in Mississippi parallels that of the Chickasaw, the Creeks in Alabama, and the Cherokee. All of the southeastern tribes underwent much the same acculturation process, and all suffered the eventual consequence of tribal disunity and removal.

The central theme in the story of southeastern Indian history during the years prior to removal is that of change from within. This fact in no way absolves the U.S. government of blame for removal or for the physical and psychological misery inflicted upon so many thousands of displaced southeastern American Indians. It does indicate, however, that removal was not simply a reflection of the Jacksonian mentality but rather evolved over several generations with the complicity of several presidents and progressed with the willing consent of many important tribal members.

Notes

1. The French colonizers of the Gulf Coast in the early eighteenth century, for example, had a strong penchant for the native girls, an appetite that the accompanying Jesuits roundly criticized (Charles L. Sullivan, *The Mississippi Gulf Coast: Portrait of a People* [Northridge, Calif.: Windsor Publications, 1985], 15).

2. Angie Debo, *The Rise and Fall of the Choctaw Republic*, 2d ed. (Norman: University of Oklahoma Press, 1961); Robert Cotterill, *The Southern Indians* (Norman: University of Oklahoma Press, 1954); Francis Paul Prucha, *American Indian Policy in the Formative Years: The Indian Trade and Intercourse Acts, 1790-1834* (Cambridge, Mass.: Harvard University Press, 1962).

3. Arthur DeRosier, Jr., *The Removal of the Choctaw Indians* (Knoxville: University of Tennessee Press, 1970); W. David Baird, *Peter Pitchlynn: Chief of the Choctaws* (Norman: University of Oklahoma Press, 1972); Arrell M. Gibson, *The Chickasaws* (Norman: University of Oklahoma Press, 1971); Horatio Cushman, *History of the Choctaw, Chickasaw, and Natchez Indians* (1899; reprint, New York: Russell and Russell, 1972).

Thomas P. Abernethey, *The Formative Period in Alabama, 1815-1828* (n.p., 1922), 9-10.

5. Samuel J. Wells, "Counting Countrymen on the Tombigbee," *Southern Historian* 4 (Spring 1983): 2-11.

6. This problem has concerned mainly anthropologists. Historians tend to use the

term that was used during the period under study, in this case, "half-breed" or "mixed-blood." In the author's opinion, "mixed-blood" is the more acceptable term.

7. Buckingham Smith, trans., *Narratives of the Career of Hernando de Soto* (New York, Allerton Book Co., 1922), pp. 27–34; John Grier Varner and Jeanette Johnson Varner, eds. and trans., *The Florida of the Inca* (Austin: Univ. of Texas Press, 1951), p. 93.

8. Mississippi Department of Archives and History (hereafter MDAH), Territorial Governor's Records, Record Group 2, folder 7, item 432, Pitchlynn to Dinsmoor, January 27, 1805; Samuel J. Wells, "Rum, Skins, and Powder: A Choctaw Interpreter and the Treaty of Mount Dexter," *Chronicles of Oklahoma* 61, no. 4 (Winter 1983–84): 422–28.

9. Cushman, *History of the Choctaw*, 35–36. For an insight into diplomacy involving the Choctaw tribe during this period, see Patricia Kay Galloway, ed., "Minutes of Council with Choctaws," *Mississippi Provincial Archives, French Dominion, 1749–1763* (Baton Rouge: LSU Press, 1984), 5:213–22, 294–301.

10. Charles C. Royce, *Indian Land Cessions and the United States*, Eighteenth Annual Report of the U.S. Bureau of American Ethnology, 1896–97 (Washington, D.C.: Government Printing Office, 1899), 359.

11. One of the most influential British companies was Panton, Leslie and Company, which operated out of Mobile and Pensacola with the blessing of the Spanish authorities. This organization figured prominently in several treaties with the Choctaw and Creeks.

12. James M. Crawford, *The Mobilian Trade Language* (Knoxville: University of Tennessee Press, 1978), 30; Kenneth H. York, "Mobilian: The Indian *Lingua Franca* of Colonial Louisiana," in *La Salle and His Legacy: Frenchmen and Indians in the Lower Mississippi Valley*, ed. Patricia K. Galloway (Jackson: University Press of Mississippi, 1983), 140.

13. Juzan family genealogies on file in MDAH indicate that Pierre, the first of the family in the New World, had a military commission from the French king.

14. Charles Hudson, *The Southeastern Indians* (Knoxville: University of Tennessee Press, 1976), 188; The presence of "half-breeds" in Choctaw country was documented not long after the Treaty of San Lorenzo; see "Choctaw Deputation to Commissioners of the United States," December 15, 1801, *American State Papers: Indian Affairs*, 1, p. 662.

15. Cushman, *History of the Choctaw*, 499.

16. Ibid., 331; Baird, *Peter Pitchlynn*, 7; Albert J. Pickett, *History of Alabama and Incidentally of Georgia and Mississippi*, 2 vols. (1851; reprint, Sheffield, Ala.: R. C. Randolph, 1896), 469–70. Pickett reports operational cotton gins in Indian country as early as 1802. One was erected on the Tombigbee not far north of present-day Columbus, Mississippi, and was named Cotton Gin Port.

17. Cushman, *History of the Choctaw*, 343–44; The success of Greenwood Leflore is more impressive in light of the near illiteracy of the letters that he wrote just before removal. Leflore to McKenny, May 5, 1828, Letters Received by the Office of Indian Affairs, 1824–1871, Record Group 75, National Archives, microfilm M-234.

18. Ibid., 331. Choctaw mixed-blood Nathaniel Folsom also identifies mixed-blood Hardy Perry as the man who first introduced cattle raising into the eastern part of the Choctaw Nation.

19. Ibid., 275–76.

20. Ibid., 318; Folsom exercised his influence on the tribe and the American officials as early as 1816 when he requested, during negotiations at the Treaty of the Choctaw Trading House, that certain Choctaw mixed-bloods be granted land reservations east of the Tombigbee River. "Extracts. . . ," October 24, 1816, *American State Papers: Indian Affairs*, 1, p. 122.

21. Baird, *Peter Pitchlynn*, 6–12; MDAH, Record Group 2, vol. 24, folder 7, item 432.

22. Contemporary observers in 1786 described John Pitchlynn as young and sober and "in the Nation twelve years." "The Choctaws," January 4, 1786, *American State Papers: Indian Affairs*, 7, pp. 58–59; also see Charles Hudson, *The Southeastern Indians*, for an interesting discussion of clans and kinships, 184–202.

23. This theory was formulated by the late Richard S. Lackey, fellow, American Genealogical Society.

24. MDAH, Subject Files.

25. Douglas H. Ubelaker, "The Sources and Methodology for Mooney's Estimates of North American Indian Populations," in *The Native Population of the Americas in 1492*, ed. William M. Denevan (Madison: University of Wisconsin Press, 1976), 262–63. Ubelaker agreeds that there were about 4,000–5,000 Choctaw households before removal but estimates the total population at only 15,000. Nathaniel Folsom estimated the preremoval population at 30,000 (Cushman, *History of the Choctaw*, 329). A check of the preremoval census, known as the Armstrong Roll, yields well over 1,000 non-Indian names of heads of household.

26. National Archives, Records of the Bureau of Indian Affairs, Record Group 75, T-494, Treaty of Dancing Rabbit Creek. Four American treaties negotiated between 1786 and 1803 had only 1 mixed-blood signer, while the Treaty of Mount Dexter in 1805 included 9 mixed-bloods among the 23 signers. The Treaty of the Choctaw Trading House in 1816 had 2 mixed-bloods in 13 signers; the Treaty of Doak's Stand in 1820 had 25 mixed-bloods in the 103 signers; the Treaty of Washington in 1825 had 4 mixed bloods in 8 signers. Thus the ratio of mixed-blood to full-blood signers rose unevenly until the signing of the removal treaty at Dancing Rabbit Creek, when it became necessary to obtain as large a slate of signatures as possible in order to give the Choctaw Nation the most solid removal front that could be constructed.

27. For examples of this voluminous source material, see *American State Papers: Public Lands*, 8, Doc. 1523, 686; "Gaines' Reminiscences," typescript, MDAH, Z431f.; Dreisback to Draper, July 1874, Draper Collection, Series U, Wisconsin Historical Society, microfilm; Miscellaneous Choctaw Removal Records, Entry 267, Record Group 75, Records of the Bureau of Indian Affairs, National Archives; Choctaw Census Roll (Armstrong Roll), ibid., 1831, Entry 258; Choctaw Census Roll (Cooper Roll) of Those Remaining East of the Mississippi, 1856, ibid., Entry 260.

28. David Folsom to William Ward, November 7, 1829, Letters Received by Office of Indian Affairs, 1824–1881, Record Group 75, National Archives, microfilm M-234.

29. Commissioners to Barbour, November 19, 1826, *American State Papers: Indian Affairs*, 2, p. 709. For an earlier assessment of mixed-bloods' influence on the tribe, see McKee to Jackson, August 13, 1819, *American State Papers: Indian Affairs*, 2, p. 280, and Commissioners to Choctaw Nation, October 3, 1820, ibid., 234.

30. Herman J. Viola, *Thomas L. McKenny, Architect of America's Early Indian Policy: 1816–1830* (Chicago: University of Chicago Press, 1974), 40–46, 126–34; To the Congress of the United States, February 18, 1825, *American State Papers: Indian Affairs*, 2, pp. 528–59.

31. Debo, *Rise and Fall*, 59–60.

4

Chief Greenwood Leflore
and His Malmaison Plantation

R. Halliburton, Jr.

Among the Choctaw who did not emigrate to Indian Territory during the nineteenth century, Greenwood Leflore, a Mississippi Choctaw mixed-blood, is the most famous. His story begins in 1792, when the French Canadian voyageur Louis Le Fleur arrived at Mobile in the French province of Louisiana. Louis Le Fleur soon established friendly relations with the Indians in the surrounding area, began trading with them, and established trading posts in the present-day state of Mississippi. One of his trading stations was called Le Fleur's Bluff and was situated near the present city of Jackson. Le Fleur married Rebecca Cravat, a mixed-blood Choctaw, and on June 3, 1800, Greenwood Le Fleur was born.[1] The young Le Fleur was named Greenwood after an English sea captain, a friend and former partner of the elder Le Fleur.

When Greenwood was about twelve years old, his father operated a trading post and tavern on the old Natchez Trace at a point still known as French Camp. A mail carrier named Major John Donley made regular deliveries between Nashville and Natchez, passing the Le Fleur establishment. Donley was impressed by the youthful Greenwood, who could not speak a word of English. With the parents' approval, he brought Greenwood to his Nashville home to attend school.[2]

Young Le Fleur remained in the Donley home for six years, and during that time he fell in love with Donley's daughter, Rosa. He told Major Donley of his love for Rosa and his wish to marry her. Both

56

Greenwood Leflore, shown here circa 1835, became an influential planter and member of Mississippi's non-Indian community. *Courtesy of the Mississippi Department of Archives and History*

parents objected to the union because they considered Greenwood and Rosa too young. Some time later, Greenwood specifically asked Major Donley, "Sir, if you loved a beautiful maiden and her parents objected to the marriage, what would you do?" Donley reportedly replied, "I would steal the girl and marry her, anyway." Greenwood Le Fleur proceeded to "steal" Rosa and married her in about 1820. Guests at the wedding ceremony, held in his father's plantation home, included many of Mississippi's elite.[3]

At about this time young Le Fleur changed the spelling of his surname to Leflore, settled in Mississippi, and rapidly gained prominence and position among his people. Some people called him as "ambitious as Lucifer." He became a planter and by the middle 1820s was accumulating black slaves to till his fields. At the age of twenty-two, Leflore was chosen to be chief of the Western district of the Choctaw Nation. At the Great Council of March 15, 1830, he was elected chief of the entire nation.[4]

Leflore became a progressive influence within his tribe, initiating many reforms among his people. He urged the Choctaw to find permanent residences and to take up cultivation of the land; helped establish schools; and encouraged his people to send their children to be educated. He suppressed numerous tribal rights and customs that he considered backward. He prohibited the charms and sorceries of medicine men, advocated civil marriage ceremonies, opposed divorces, and encouraged Christianity. He was also instrumental in repealing the ancient unwritten law of blood for blood and abolished the custom of raising poles over the graves of the dead.[5]

After negotiation of the Treaty of Dancing Rabbit Creek, which he signed, Leflore became increasingly unpopular with his people. He was eventually deposed as chief in favor of his nephew, George W. Harkins. When his people crossed the Mississippi River and headed for their new home in the West, Greenwood Leflore remained in Mississippi. The U.S. government had previously awarded him a thousand acres of land and had conferred upon him the military title of colonel for his "services." When he was accused of accepting a bribe from the U.S. government to sign the removal treaty, he reportedly replied, "Which is worse, for a great government to offer a bribe or a poor Indian to take one?"[6]

Chief Greenwood Leflore

Leflore now owned a large plantation and regularly purchased additional slaves from members of his family, neighbors, and slave dealers. His largest purchase was 100 blacks, whom he bought from an estate in 1839. By this time he owned thousands of acres of fertile land in the heart of the Mississippi delta. Leflore reportedly never separated families or sold slaves unless they proved to be unmanageable. Although he may never have sold members of families separately, however, his records indicate that he usually purchased slaves singly or in twos and that most of them were young. A number of these slaves must have been separated from their relatives.[7]

In about 1850 many cotton planters entered a golden age, and it became fashionable to build splendid mansions in keeping with their wealth and station. About this time, James C. Harris, an architect and well-known builder from Georgia, appeared in Mississippi. Harris was a specialist in the construction of palatial plantation houses. These houses were usually built of wood, the heavy timbers hewed by hand and the other lumber purchased from local or nearby sawmills. A gang of trained slave builders and artisans did the actual construction under Harris's supervision. The slaves accomplished the most delicate interior finishing, carving, and decorative paneling as well as the less exacting but heavier work of framing.[8]

Greenwood Leflore had long dreamed of possessing a "wondrous manor house," and in 1854 he arranged for James Harris to build it. Leflore had been a lifelong admirer of Napoleon Bonaparte and his wife, Josephine. Even though she was divorced, Josephine continued to be Leflore's heroine, like Joan of Arc a martyr to man's inhumanity. Leflore christened his home "Malmaison," the "House of Sorrow," after the chateau ten miles west of Paris on the Seine where Josephine lived the last sixteen years of her life.[9]

Greenwood Leflore's Malmaison was the largest house ever erected in Carrol County. All the lumber was cut from his own lands, was sawed at his own steam-powered sawmill, and was transported to the building site by his wagon teams of oxen driven by slaves. The cypress sills were hand hewn and were stored above ground for one year to season. The bricks for the foundation, walks, six fireplaces and chimneys, two large cisterns, and a smokehouse were molded and fired by Leflore's slaves in his own kilns. The house was an imposing two-story edifice built in

Malmaison as it appeared early in the twentieth century. *Photo: R. Halliburton, Jr.*

the "favorite style of architecture of the 'Old South,'" with wide galleries, many balconies, wrought iron balustrades, lofty chambers, spacious hallways, and beautiful hand-carved oak paneling. A picturesque observatory surrounded by a walkway and ornamental railing adorned the roof and afforded a spectacular view of the valleys, hills, and river.[10]

Malmaison contained fifteen rooms, eight of which measured twenty by twenty-five feet and had ceilings fifteen feet high. The best French and English decorators were brought from New Orleans to decorate the house. Most of the furnishings for the great house were imported from France. The silver, embossed with wild roses, and the monogrammed crystal and china came in sets of twelve dozen pieces. The silver and glassware were reportedly valued at $150,000. The thirty-by-sixty-foot dining room contained a butler's pantry, where the tableware "were carefully washed by slaves and checked by the head slave." The furniture, constructed in France by special order, was mostly of hickory and was overlaid with gold—not gilt—with upholstery of crimson silk damask. The marvelous Louis XIV drawing room set of thirty pieces was fashioned from solid mahogany, finished in gold, and reportedly cost $10,000. The Duchess of Orleans attempted to purchase the set before it was shipped to Mississippi and, failing to do so, ordered a duplicate made for herself.[11]

Other furnishings included oil canvases from the hands of masters, family portraits by Benjamin West, beautiful mirrors in gold frames, tables, large four-poster beds of rosewood with silk and satin canopies, and four tapestry window curtains depicting the four palaces of Napoleon and Josephine—Versailles, Malmaison, Saint Cloud, and Fontainebleau. A rosewood piano graced the entrance hall, and gun closets and ammunition chests flanked the front door, which was ornamented with silver hardware. There were eleven black Italian marble mantels. The parlor was lighted with a golden candelabra that burned whale oil. All interior doors were ten feet high, three feet wide, and two and one-half inches thick. The floors were unstained, random-width planks beautifully carpeted.[12]

A detached kitchen stood some fifty feet from the house but was connected to it by a covered veranda. The kitchen contained two huge double fireplaces with cranes placed at various levels for cooking. The ceiling of each room held bell cords attached to bells in the servants' quarters. The bell for each room had a separate and distinct tone, allowing the slaves to know which room required service. Fine wines were aged in a cellar under the carriage house and were later stored in wine closets under the staircases of the house[13]

Malmaison and its furnishings were designed to accommodate and entertain 200 guests at a time. Large numbers of trained servants were therefore needed, and Leflore spared no expense to obtain them. In 1857 he purchased an eighteen-year-old mulatto girl as a servant for his wife, paying $1,800. One of the most memorable gala events held at Malmaison was the wedding of Greenwood Leflore's daughter, Rebecca, to James Harris, the architect of the house. The bride received lavish gifts, including a plantation and 100 slaves to operate it.[14]

A large gate admitted guests to the beautifully landscaped grounds, which had handsome formal gardens and a miniature lake with swans, geese, and many varieties of ornamental fish. Holly, mimosa, boxwood, magnolia, jasmine, pine, cedar, and live oak trees graced the grounds.

R. HALLIBURTON, JR.

A stream near the mansion was dammed and stocked with game fish, and the plantation had its own wild game reserve. Two guests houses provided ample space for the numerous visitors to Malmaison. The Leflore family rode in a coach with a slave driver in livery. The coach was upholstered in tufted satin damask held in place by ivory tacks and illuminated by lamps of silver and cut crystal. Leflore once traveled all the way to Washington in the coach for a conference with President Andrew Jackson.[15]

Malmaison stood approximately fourteen miles east of the present city of Greenwood, Mississippi. It eventually grew to more than 15,000 acres of fertile delta land and was worked by 400 slaves. Cotton, corn, and other crops were grown in great quantities, and the plantation was immensely profitable. The principal crop was cotton, which was ginned and baled on the plantation and was then shipped aboard Leflore's own steamboat.[16]

Greenwood Leflore represented his county in the Mississippi House of Representatives for two terms and then served one term in the state senate. As a senator Leflore was constantly exasperated by his colleagues' use of Latin in their speeches. A young senator once made an entire speech in Latin. Leflore afterward rose and began speaking in Choctaw. He continued for an hour. When he had finished, he asked the senators which speech had been better understood.[17]

As the Civil War approached, Leflore spoke against secession and warned his listeners that it would put their wives and daughters in the kitchen and at the washtub. Leflore's enemies once set fire to Malmaison, but slaves quickly extinguished the flames. When the war began, Leflore remained loyal to the Union. He refused to recognize the Confederacy and would not pay taxes to its government. One of his slaves was seized and was sold to satisfy his Confederate tax debt, but friends paid the taxes and returned the servant to his master.

During the war Greenwood Leflore lost his cotton, all of his slaves, and much other valuable property. He died a natural death at Malmaison on August 21, 1865, and is interred in the family cemetery on the grounds. A great-granddaughter, Nola Leflore Brown, who was born at Malmaison in 1888, now lives in Tahlequah, Oklahoma. The federal government once attempted to purchase Malmaison in order to restore it as a historic landmark. The Leflore family refused to sell the mansion, however, and continued to occupy it. Malmaison was never modernized but survived until March 31, 1942, when it was completely destroyed by a fire of undetermined origin. Only a few pieces of silver and crystal and some chairs were saved from destruction.[18]

Notes

1. "Malmaison and Its Memories," archives of the Choctaw Agency of the Bureau of Indian Affairs, Philadelphia, Mississippi (this ten-page document is hereafter cited as Choctaw Agency manuscript), 2; Mary Garland Barton Ingram, "Malmaison, Home of Greenwood Leflore," Indian Archives, Oklahoma Historical Society, Oklahoma City (this thirteen-page document is hereafter cited as Malmaison manuscript), 2–3; Angie Debo, *The Rise and Fall of the Choctaw Republic*, 2d ed. (Norman: University of Oklahoma Press, 1961), 58.
2. Choctaw Agency manuscript, 3; Malmaison manuscript, 3.
3. Choctaw Agency manuscript, 3–4; Leflore was a Methodist.
4. Ibid.
5. Ibid., 6; Malmaison manuscript, 4.
6. Choctaw Agency manuscript, 5; Mrs. N. D. Deupree, "Greenwood Leflore," *Publications of the Mississippi Historical Society* 7 (1903):146.
7. Charles S. Sydnor, *Slavery in Mississippi* (Baton Rouge: Louisiana State University Press, 1966), 131–33.
8. Choctaw Agency manuscript, 6–7; Malmaison manuscript, 6.
9. Choctaw Agency manuscript, 7; Malmaison manuscript, 6.
10. Mrs. Lee J. Langley, "Malmaison: Place in a Wilderness, Home of General Leflore," *Chronicles of Oklahoma* 5, no. 4 (December 1927):372; Malmaison manuscript, 7.
11. Phil Harris, "Malmaison—The Mansion of Leflore," *Muskogee Sunday Phoenix and Times–Democrat*, October 12, 1975; Langley, "Malmaison," 372.
12. Malmaison manuscript, 8–10.
13. Ibid., 13.
14. Ibid.; Sydnor, *Slavery in Mississippi*, 131.
15. Malmaison manuscript, 10.
16. Deupree, "Greenwood Leflore," 146; Thelma V. Bounds, *Children of Nanih Waiya* (San Antonio: Naylor, 1964), 42.
17. Deupree, "Greenwood Leflore," 150; Langley, "Malmaison," 379.
18. *Memphis Press Scimitar*, April 2, 1942.

5

The Choctaw Struggle for Land and Identity in Mississippi, 1830–1918

Clara Sue Kidwell

In September of 1830, a small number of leaders of the Choctaw tribe signed the Treaty of Dancing Rabbit Creek, by which the tribe ceded all claims to its lands in the state of Mississippi and agreed to move to an area west of the Mississippi River that had been guaranteed to the Choctaw by a treaty in 1820. Because of the resistance of many members of the tribe, however, Article 14 was inserted in the treaty so that members of the tribe who wished to stay in Mississippi could become citizens of the state and could claim individual allotments of land. For those who wished to remove, Article 19 provided that Choctaw farmers who had homes and fields could take land claims. It was envisioned that they would be able to sell their claims to white settlers moving into the old Choctaw territory and would thus have money to reestablish themselves in their new homes. Finally, some individuals who were specifically recognized by the U.S. government were awarded allotments of land.[1]

The treaty provision for allotments of land shows the tragic choice that confronted individual Choctaw. They could remain in their homeland not as Choctaw but as citizens of the state of Mississippi, or they could maintain their tribal allegiance and relinquish their homes to move to the new territory west of the Mississippi River.

The issue of land and identity is a very important one for the Choctaw. The decisions that were forced upon them by the U.S. government are important for the identity of the contemporary Mississippi Choctaw people. The history of the development of the public lands in the United States—tracts owned by the government—is an essential part of the history of the United States. The availability of public lands made it possible for white settlers to move into territory that had previously been occupied by Indian nations. As Indian lands were opened and white settlers moved in, the lives of both peoples underwent significant changes. The Choctaw people in Mississippi after 1830 waged a major struggle to preserve their claims to their native lands, and their presence in Mississippi today attests to their efforts.

The Choctaw agent in 1830, William Ward, was instructed to register the claims of individual Choctaw under the fourteenth article. The treaty provided that claims must be registered within six months of the ratification of the treaty by the Senate, that is, by August 24, 1831.[2] The instructions to begin the registration, however, did not reach Ward until June of 1831. Many individuals who wanted to file for individual claims found their intentions deliberately thwarted by Ward, who appears to have been an incompetent drunkard.[3]

Of the applicants for allotments, Ward transmitted to the War Department the names of only sixty-nine heads of family, of whom fifteen were white men with Choctaw wives and twenty-four were mixed bloods.[4] The register also indicated 152 children under the age of ten (who were entitled to receive 160 acres) and 77 children over ten (who were entitled to 320 acres).[5] The census of Choctaw eligible for claims under the nineteenth article was compiled by F. W. Armstrong and listed more than 14,000 people (heads of family and their children).[6]

On June 26, 1833, George W. Martin was appointed by the government to select the tracts to be granted to individual Choctaw under the provisions of Articles 14, 15, and 19. Confirmation of the Choctaw claims was necessary before the public sale of the cession could proceed. As Martin began his task he found, first of all, that a set of plat maps of the ceded lands would not be available to him because the General Land Office was preparing copies for the pending public land sales.[7] He then found that Ward's register of claimants was only an imperfect copy. The original had been sent to Washington, and Ward could not attest to the accuracy of the copies that he gave to Martin.[8] Martin was also under pressure to complete his task before the public land sales of Choctaw lands in October.[9]

CLARA SUE KIDWELL

In locating the Choctaw claims, Martin found himself faced with difficult decisions. The fourteenth article called for 640-acre tracts, laid out along sectional lines, to include the improvements (cleared fields, houses, fences, and so forth) of the Indian. Some improvements crossed the lines, however, and there were also competing claims. The government was insisting on self-sufficient farms for people who had traditionally lived in villages consisting of scattered houses surrounded by fields. The spacing of houses in the village did not allow a full 640-acre plot to be included with each.[10] When Martin could not include the full amount of land, he was instructed to locate other land of equal value for the claimant.

When Choctaw land entered the public domain as a result of the treaty, its value was set by Congress at $1.25 an acre. The potential value of the land was much greater because many people wanted to move into Mississippi. Land that was bought cheaply could be sold for much higher prices, and speculation in public lands was rampant. White people who wanted to acquire Indian land at cheap prices and to resell it at higher prices began to travel among the Choctaw people. In many cases, they contracted with the Indians and agreed to act as agents, putting forward the Indians' claims in exchange for a portion of the land that they were awarded.

As Martin traveled in the Choctaw cession, he heard complaints from individuals that their claims had not been properly registered by Ward. He evidently did not take these complaints very seriously because he personally felt that there had been many efforts to press spurious claims through his office. He expressed frustration that he had been unable to obtain proper land maps of the ceded lands and complained to Secretary of War Lewis Cass on December 6 of having had to ride long distances to procure maps from the district land offices as surveys were completed. He also spoke of his inability to locate all the claims properly.[11]

On October 13, 1834, Martin received a letter from Mahlon Dickerson, the acting secretary of war, indicating that the department had received claims for reservations from people who indicated that Ward had not registered their names or had registered them and had then lost the pages on which they were listed. Dickerson instructed Martin to give public notice that persons who felt they had claims could come forth with evidence.[12] On October 13, 1834, President Andrew Jackson authorized Martin to remove from public sale the lands claimed by Choctaw who came forward with evidence that their names had been excluded from the register through the mistakes or neglect of the agent. The location of the lands, however, was to be contingent upon the sanction of Congress. Until Congress acted, the locations would be reserved from sale but would not be assigned to the claimants.[13]

When Martin filed his lists of the Choctaw claims with the War Department in August 1834, he indicated that many reserves remained to be located because maps were not available.[14] In December of that year, he also filed documents containing the testimony of men supporting the statements of several Choctaw that their claims had not been properly registered by the agent.[15]

Most of the claims related to the council held in June 1831, at which the tribal annuities were to be distributed. The testimony presented to Martin was a veritable catalog of acts by William Ward and by white men in Mississippi that had led to the dispossession of the Choctaw. According to Grabel Lincecum, when a leader of the Choctaw living on the Pearl, Leaf, and Suckenatchee rivers had brought forward a bundle of sticks representing the claims of individual Indians, Ward took them, threw them away, and told the Indians that there were too many of them and that they must move west.[16] The testimony indicated that Ward had actively discouraged the claims and that he was drunk during many of the proceedings. He rejected or destroyed a large number of applications, telling the Indians to emigrate instead. It was established that he had lost pages of the register containing the names of claimants.[17]

Ward had explained his actions in rejecting claims in a letter to an official at the Choctaw Agency in June 1831, when he said he felt that the actions of the Indians in filing claims were often incited by white men and that he was only carrying out government policy in urging the Indians to move west.[18] Whether Ward felt that he was legitimately carrying out federal policy by rejecting claims, whether he was justifying his drunkenness and incompetence, or both, his actions had a tremendous impact on the Choctaw who remained in Mississippi. His failure to register people who desired allotments continued to jeopardize the Indians' rights.

In addition to the complaints and testimony that Martin presented, several Choctaw protested directly in a memorial to Congress. They noted that their ceded lands were being opened to public settlement before the outstanding Indian claims under Article 14 of the Treaty of Dancing Rabbit Creek had been fully settled. The memorialists were Moontubbee Annouchi, Hopah-cha-nubbee, Little Leader, and Red Post Oak. These men said that a number of Indians had gone to the agent at various times to register and that he had written down their names but that their names did not appear on the final register he gave to George Martin. Seeking justice, they rejected the proposal that they be given money instead of the land that had been promised them.[19]

Charges were made by Mississippi citizens to the Congress of the United States that white land speculators had gone among the Choctaw during 1830–1831 to encourage them to stay in Mississippi and to take allotments. The speculators contracted with the Choctaw people so that they would receive rights to half the land the people claimed. Many congressmen and citizens of Mississippi were defeating the purpose of the treaty by keeping the Choctaw in Mississippi, but the speculators rather than the Indians would profit.[20]

By 1836 probably 5,000 Choctaw remained in Mississippi. Between the winter of 1831–1832 and 1836, approximately 14,000 of the 19,554 Choctaw on the census of claimants under the nineteenth article had moved west. Those who remained had secured no official government recognition as Indians nor any tribal land base. They remained as potential claimants, however, to the public lands in the state of Mississippi.[21]

There was debate in the Congress as to how to deal with Choctaw claims. On March 22, 1836, the Committee on Private Land Claims recommended that action on pending claims be taken by Congress directly. The report stated that the Indians had originally lived on the poorest land and that, when the land had been sold, more valuable land had been assigned. Approval of Indian claims would benefit the land speculators who pressed Indian claims in exchange for part of the land awarded. It would not benefit the Indian claimants.[22] Congress decided however, that the only way to address the problem was to appoint a commission to investigate the situation.[23] This action suspended the claims that Martin had already located.

On March 3, 1837, Congress created a commission to deal with claims under the Article 14 of the Treaty of Dancing Rabbit Creek that had not been satisfied by Martin's locations on the basis of Ward's registers. The commission would hear evidence and would determine whether claimants had fulfilled the provisions of the fourteenth article—they had signified their intent to register, they had lived on the land for five years thereafter, and they had made improvements. The act specifically forbade the approval of claims involving an Indian who was raising the child of another person as his own. This provision indicates a certain ethnocentrism in Congress, since the Choctaw children were often brought up by people who were not their natural parents. Furthermore, the act in no way approved the contingent locations George Martin had made on the basis of Indian claims.[24]

Although Congress did not approve any of the claims, they plainly had to be settled before public land sales in Mississippi could proceed, because charges of speculation called into doubt the legitimacy of land sales in the Choctaw cession. The commissioners faced several problems. Did the Choctaw claimants have a valid right to their land, having fulfilled the requirements of the Treaty of Dancing Rabbit Creek? Were their claims, valid or not, inspired by greedy land speculators? If the claims were indeed valid, who would benefit, the Choctaw or the white land speculators and lawyers who represented the claims only because they stood to receive a portion of the land awarded?

The commissioners appointed were P.D. Vroom, former governor of New Jersey, Publius R. R. Pray, and James R. Murray. They opened an office in Columbus, Mississippi, on June 22, 1837, and drew up a notice to be published in the newspapers of the area advertising a call for claims. They decided to begin hearings on October 16.[25] Their first meeting, however, was not held until November 6, and hearings did not begin until January 1, 1838, at Leflore's place, where Murray and Vroom were joined by Roger Barton, who had replaced Pray. By March 1, the commissioners reported having heard testimony in 175 claims. They estimated that there would be a total of 800 or 900.[26]

Because of the initial delays, the number of claims to be heard, and the fact that the legislation establishing the commission expired on March 1, 1838, congress extended the life of the commission in the act of February 2, 1838.[27]

On March 27, 1838, the commissioners began hearings at Louisville,

Mississippi. The complaints were similar to those gathered by George Martin—that William Ward had refused to register claims and that he had treated the register carelessly. Ward was also said to have discouraged the Indians by telling them that the law of Mississippi would be imposed upon them. Although various groups had designated spokesmen, Ward had refused to take the lists they presented.

A number of the claims in which the commissioners heard testimony were represented by Charles Fisher, whose examination of witnesses was designed to elicit testimony of Ward's drunkeness and incompetence. At one point, testimony revealed that Ward had personally disliked Little Leader, one of the Choctaw who had written Congress in protest. The U.S. attorney asked whether any of the claimants had gone west and then returned, which would have negated their claims. The witnesses denied that such was the case.

Some of the evidence presented to the commission called into question the role of land speculators. One witness testified that he had been employed by Daniel Wright, Charles Fisher, and Doctor Gwin to locate Indian lands. Although he had no knowledge that they had specific financial interests in these lands, the fact that the three men had formed a company for speculation invited consideration of the role that these individuals might play in the claims.[28]

The commissioners adjourned on May 14, 1838. On July 31, Murray and Vroom submitted the final results of their hearings to the president. Although the legislation governing the commission was very stringent in its conditions for establishing the legitimacy of the claims, the commissioners were sympathetic to the situation of the claimants. They noted that the Indians had a deep attachment to their land:

> Their known attachment to their homes, the councils held by them on the subject, and their constant declarations of their intention to remain and take the benefit of the treaty, have not been without their influence in bringing the board to the conclusion that it was the most universal intention of these Indians now remaining east of the Mississippi to take the benefit of the 14th art. of the treaty.[29]

The commissioners reported decisions on 261 of the claims before them, of which 165 were judged valid, 65 were rejected, 26 were recommended favorably for action by Congress, and 5 were unfinished. The cases they recommended favorably included instances in which children were being raised by adults who were not their natural parents. The commissioners noted that this was Choctaw custom.[30]

The commissioners, however, acted on only a small number of the 1,349 claims by heads of families that were laid before them, which, together with the 77 claims that had actually been registered by William Ward, made a total of 1,426 Choctaw claims that remained on public land in Mississippi.[31]

Murray and Vroom noted in their report:

> The Choctaw Indians are shy and reserved in their intercourse with the whites, and do not readily mix with them; it is proved in a great number of cases that they have been most wantonly abused and ill-treated . . . The large stocks of cattle and hogs introduced by the white settlers destroyed their crops, and their houses and cabins were torn down, burned, or taken possession of by them, when they left home on their necessary hunting expeditions, or to seek employment in picking cotton, &c . . . Many removed in consequence of reports circulated among them that the lands occupied by them had been sold by the government, and when it was impossible for them to ascertain the truth or falsehood of such reports; they well knew, however, from bitter experience, that, whether true or false, they were at the mercy of their white neighbors.[32]

Since the recommendations of the commission concerning claims awaited the final approval of Congress, the title to much of the land in Mississippi was still unclear. Congress had failed to act on George Martin's original locations of land for the Choctaw and had instead created a commission. The commission for several reasons failed to act definitively on the recommendations made by its commissioners. First, because the laws establishing the commission had expired before all the claims could be investigated and decided, the matter was far from settled. Second, and probably most important, there were still suspicions that Choctaw claimants had not lived and made improvements on the land that they were now claiming. The Indians were believed to be at the mercy of land speculators who were encouraging them to claim lands that the speculators would ultimately receive.

Since Congress did not act on the recommendations of Murray and Vroom, and much of the land in the Choctaw cession had been sold, the government was left in a quandary as to how to settle the Choctaw claims. On March 9, 1842, J.C. Spencer, secretary of war, wrote to the chairman of the Senate Committee on Indian Affairs, indicating that approximately 225,000 acres of land had been selected to satisfy Choctaw claims and that approximately 226,000 more acres would have to be set aside to satisfy claims approved by Murray and Vroom. Although the approximately 7,796,000 acres that had been ceded in the Treaty of

Dancing Rabbit Creek represented sufficient land, much of it had been sold to the public already, and Spencer doubted that Choctaw claims could be satisfied with land. He recommended instead that the value of the land be given to Choctaw claimants in money.[33]

The Choctaw commission was revived on August 23, 1842, to deal with the situation of claims.[34] The law reviving the commission made a significant change in the situation. Because of the delays in action, much of the land in question had already been sold. Where the tracts claimed by Choctaw and approved by the commission had been sold at public sale, Indians were to be allowed to select territory from the public domain in Mississippi, Louisiana, Alabama, and Arkansas. The Choctaw were, furthermore, to be issued scrip (certificates of claims) that they could exchange for public lands. Their claims were thus to be paid off in paper certificates. The law also provided, however, that only half the certificate was to be issued in Mississippi. The claimant would receive the other half after removal to the Choctaw territory west of the Mississippi. The law also gave the commission authority over claims under both the fourteenth article and the nineteenth. It explicitly denied the approval of claims which had been assigned to other parties before the five-year occupancy requirement had been satisfied. This section of the act obviously responded to the charges that lawyers had contracted with Indians to represent their claims in exchange for part of the land they would receive. The act also shifted the authority for final confirmation of claims from congress to the president.[35]

The commission of 1837 was created to establish the legitimacy of Choctaw claims, and the commissioners responded sympathetically to the Indians' situation. The act of 1842 makes it clear that Congress intended to ensure the removal of the Choctaw remaining in Mississippi. The substitution of scrip for land patents served to deprive the Indians of their rights. There was no way that the Choctaw who wished to remain in Mississippi could do so without relinquishing their claims to land.

Three Mississippians were selected for the 1842 commission: John F. H. Claiborne of Natchez, Ralph Graves of Columbus, and Roger Barton of Holly Springs. They were instructed to begin their work on December 1, 1842, at Garlandsville.[36] They actually began hearings at Hopahka in Leake County. Later, on January 16, 1843, E. B. W.

Kirksey and James Poindexter addressed a letter to the commissioners, asserting that no more than 150 Indian heads of families were eligible for land. Kirksey and Poindexter asked that witnesses be subpoenaed to testify to that effect. They demanded that no claims be confirmed without a complete investigation. As they said, "In filing this protest, we are not actuated by any improper motive, but simply from a desire that justice should be done both to our Government, and to the Indians."[37]

Their actions led to a prompt response by Charles Fisher, the attorney who was representing Choctaw claims. He protested that the charges cast doubt on the claims of his clients and that the lack of speedy action prejudiced them further.[38]

As the exchange between Fisher and Poindexter and Kirksey indicates, the Choctaw were caught in the midst of competitors for lands in Mississippi. Fisher had represented several of the claims before the previous commission. Poindexter and Kirksey made charges of fraud, and Fisher, who had indeed made contracts with the Indians to represent their claims in exchange for land, objected to the charges.[39]

On April 1, 1843, the commissioners moved their operation to Yazoo Old Village in Neshoba County. Claiborne left for a visit with his family, leaving Graves and William Tyler of Virginia, who had replaced Barton in March, to carry on the business. One of the problems the commissioners faced concerned the claims of fathers and children. If the treaty was interpreted as giving land to the father of the children, then would the children of fathers who had gone west, leaving them behind, qualify for land? What about children of previous marriages who were often adopted into the families of maternal relatives? What about Indians who died, leaving no wills to designate heirs? Who received the land? If parts of the land covered by a family's clan were sold, were some to receive land while others were given scrip?[40]

The questions were answered by the commissioner of Indian affairs on May 15, 1843. Parents were to receive scrip on behalf of their children. If the parent's original location had been sold, his children's rights to surrounding lands could not be honored. If he had moved west, leaving behind his wife and children, their rights were forfeited.

White and Indian values conflicted at other points, for example, regarding white men who married Indian women. The treaty provided for each Choctaw head of family, and the language was interpreted to include white men who had married into the Choctaw Nation and had acquired rights therein because of Choctaw custom. The law in 1842 establishing the commission explicitly forbade claims made by white men with Indian families. The opinion of the commissioner of Indian affairs was that the more lenient construction would prevail only in decisions by the 1837 commission.[41]

The interpretation of the 1837 act was more consistent with the matrilineal tradition of Choctaw society. Men married into Choctaw families, and the offspring were accepted by the tribe. The exclusion of these white husbands by the 1842 commission represented a white distortion of Choctaw customs. Although it may have served to prevent the abuse of marriage rights by white men who only wanted Choctaw land and gained it by marriage, it conflicted with Choctaw practices regarding intermarriage. Ironically, the treaty vested rights in the male heads of families when traditional control of property had been in the hands of women and when descent in Choctaw society had passed through the mother's line. In the end, however, the male lack of eligibility often deprived women and children of their lands.

Charges that lawyers had made contracts with the Indians continued to reach the commission. In a letter of June 3, 1843, from General Reuben H. Grant, of Mississippi, to the commissioner of Indian affairs, Grant charged that the claims of Indians were fraudulent because they had made contracts to sell their land to white speculators as soon as they received it.[42]

Testimony taken by the commissioners during the course of their hearings gives a sad picture of the life of the Mississippi Choctaw during the period after 1830. In the more than 200 cases heard and recorded by Ralph Graves for the commissioners, many Choctaw testified that they had been driven from their land by white men who claimed to have bought it at public sale. Indians so dispossessed generally moved to the homes of relatives.

Despite the disruption of life caused by the forced removals, the Choctaw generally lived as they had before 1830. They raised small plots of corn and potatoes, and some still traveled west of the Mississippi to hunt, as had been a traditional custom. Families living in close proximity might cook their meals separately and eat together if they were related.[43]

The work of the commission was hampered by the conflict between Claiborne and Ralph Graves, who notified the commissioner of Indian affairs that he had suspended the hearings because of Claiborne's absence. Claiborne reacted angrily that he and Graves had agreed not to conduct business until Claiborne had returned. According to Claiborne, Graves had adopted a policy that Indians who had been dispossessed by whites would be regarded as having failed to meet the five-year residency requirement and could not claim land. Claiborne objected. Graves, on the other hand, complained that Claiborne had been eager for the board to meet at Hopahka, which "is the private residence of Colonel Forester, who is more extensively engaged as agent for the Indians than any other man in Mississippi." Graves thus implied that Claiborne was involved in land speculation himself.[44]

Again, the issue was confused between Choctaw rights to claims and the influence of land speculators on the claims. The commission appointed a special investigator to determine whether Indians had assigned their land claims to white lawyers and speculators in return for representation before the committee. The final report filed by the special agent, T. J. Word, on August 16, 1843, indicated that a number of Choctaw had assigned their claims to lawyers. Three deeds in Kemper County had been made by Opie Sketona, alias Little Leader, Ta-wam-tucha, and An-o-ka-chub-bee, conveying their lands to Daniel Gwin, John C. Whitsett, Moses Lewis, and Christopher C. Scott. Transfer of land had been made by 158 persons, "judging from the names, mostly Choctaw Indians," of one-half of their land claims. Twenty-nine of those claims were to Edward Gwin; sixty-two to Charles Fisher, William M. Gwin, Alexander F. Young, and Daniel W. Wright; and sixty-seven were to William M. Gwin and Charles Fisher.[45] Fisher, the attorney who had played so prominent a part in bringing claims before the commissions, was thus plainly a beneficiary of those claims.

Word's report substantiated the charges of speculation that had been made all along—that the Indians were not going to receive the full benefit of their claims. After the report had been filed, Claiborne made it quite clear that he considered the commission's purpose to be the removal of the Choctaw who remained in Mississippi. He proposed that the Choctaw be paid in money rather than in land for their claims.[46]

Claiborne's actions in rejecting the Choctaw claims were based not only on Word's report. There is evidence that Claiborne himself had secured his post on the commission through the political influence of William Gwin, who now stood revealed as a speculator in Choctaw lands, with the intention that he would approve the claims and would assure the success of Gwin's speculative schemes. Evidently Claiborne and Gwin had had a falling out in connection with their business dealings that led Claiborne to reject all Choctaw claims.[47]

Public opinion against the Choctaw was also generally expressed by representatives from the state of Mississippi to the secretary of war in a communication dated December 22, 1842.

> But we very much desire to have those remaining Choctaw removed at the earliest possible period. Their removal is very much called for by public opinion in Mississippi. With a view to their earliest possible removal, we most respectfully urge and request you to submit to the proper committee of the House of Representatives an estimate of the amount that will be required to effect the removal and subsistence of these Indians, to the end that an appropriation may be made at this session, and thus that the Indians may be removed as rapidly as their claims may be disposed of, and thus the State of Mississippi may be rid of this most annoying population.[48]

The law of 1842 providing scrip for the Choctaw was not repealed as Claiborne had asked but rather was used to force the Choctaw to move from Mississippi. The Choctaw commission continued to hear claims and to judge their legitimacy, but successful claimants were awarded land scrip, not the land itself.

The hearings of the commission became a fact of life for Indians in Mississippi. John McRae reported to the commissioner of Indian affairs on February 6, 1843, that as many as 1,000 Indians had gathered at Hopahka to give testimony. The Indians expected some resolution and satisfaction of their claims for land and evidently also considered the hearings a source of subsistence and perhaps even entertainment because they were fed at government expense during their stay. The Indians may have been concerned less with the satisfaction of their claims than with the chance to get free food and to socialize. McRae understood that the Choctaw claims would not be satisfied and was anxious to know what action the government would take in providing for the Indians' emigration to the western territory.[49] McRae may have been considerably more worried than the Choctaw about their own fate.

McRae informed Crawford on February 18, 1843, that he had counted 1,436 Choctaw and had enrolled 1,491 in the course of his stay. He also indicated that the commission had investigated 187 cases. He estimated that 5,000 to 6,000 Choctaw remained in the district.[50]

Although John Claiborne had withdrawn from the commission, he continued his demands that the claims be suspended. He proposed instead that the influential men among the Indians should be employed to persuade them to leave Mississippi altogether. He recommended also that the law of 1842 be repealed and that the Indians be provided with subsistence payments and scrip which they could redeem for land only after they had moved west.[51]

He described the situation of the Choctaw: "All classes and sexes are habitually intemperate, ready to barter any chattel in their possession for whiskey, and under its influence many of them have been deluded into these fraudulent assignments of their rights." He further explained: "By adopting this plan, one great object of public policy may be greatly expedited—to wit, *the removal of the Indians;* a measure called for by humanity in its loudest tones."[52]

Many Choctaw had problems associated with the use of alcohol, and Claiborne used them to justify his call for a general removal of the people from the state rather than making any attempt to improve conditions. Removal plainly freed the land that the Choctaw had ceded. Speculators who wanted to buy tracts feared that, if all the individual claims by the Choctaw were met, no land would be left for them to buy and resell at a profit.

Conflict between Claiborne and one of his fellow commissioners had already delayed the work of the commission. Now the call for suspension caused further delay and confusion. Claiborne publicly accused certain individuals of being unscrupulous land speculators and narrowly escaped a duel with one person as a result.[53]

By 1845 the Board of Choctaw Commissioners, which had continued despite Claiborne's demands, issued a report approving the claims of 143 heads of families and their children and making 1,150 Choctaw and their 2,683 children eligible for payment in scrip, half of which would be issued to them only after their removal to the west.[54]

Under pressure from public opinion in Mississippi, from the U.S. congressional delegation from the state, and from the federal government, more of the Choctaw in Mississippi made the move to Indian Territory. During the period 1845–1849, 5,120 individuals left the state. In 1853–1854, more than 600 left, and by 1860, only about 1,000 Choctaw remained in Mississippi.[55]

By 1845, the commissioners had heard 1,349 claims and had allowed 1,023. The secretary of the interior had approved 1,009 of the claims, for a total of 104,326 acres of land, and had rejected or suspended 275 claims. Claims that had still not been acted on numbered 175. Scrip for one-half of the approved claims had been issued.[56]

The decisions of the Choctaw commission led the federal government to let contracts in 1844 for the removal of the remaining Mississippi Choctaw. The contractors agreed to provide transportation and were to receive $26.715 per capita to provide food for the Indians who made the journey and $20 per capita for their subsistence for one year after their arrival in the West.[57]

Accordingly, and mindful of the amount of land that would have been needed to provide for all the claims approved by the two commissions, Congress included a provision in the Indian Appropriations Act of 1845 that the claims remaining would not be paid in scrip. Instead, the value of the lands, estimated at $1.25 per acre, would be placed in a fund bearing 5 percent interest, to be paid annually to the claimants forever.[58]

Despite continuing attempts by the federal government to remove the remaining Mississippi Choctaw, some stayed behind. In some cases the hope that their claims might eventually be recognized led the Choctaw to resist removal. Speculators encouraged their hopes, thus discouraging removal.[59] Some were willing to move to collect their subsistence payments but returned to Mississippi promptly thereafter. White men who obtained contracts to move the Indians sometimes encouraged them to return so that more money could be charged for moving them again.[60] Removal, like commission hearings, became a fact of life for some Choctaw in Mississippi.

The attempts of the government to assure the final removal of the

Choctaw were frustrated by the reluctance of the Indians themselves, by the promises of speculators that claims would be honored, and by the inventiveness of some of the Choctaw in learning to make a living from removal efforts. In 1845 the commissioner of Indian affairs in his annual report to Congress said, "It is confidently expected that before another year has gone around the Choctaws still remaining east will have joined their brethren in the western territory."[61]

During the period from November 1845 to November 1846, records show, 1,786 Choctaw moved west, "and the latest intelligence indicates that the whole emigration will be accomplished by the time limited June 30, 1847."[62] By 1847, however, "confident hopes . . . that all the Choctaws remaining east of the Mississippi would before this time, have been removed . . . have been greatly disappointed."[63] By November 1848, the commissioner was explaining that the business of removing the Choctaw had been thrown open to all persons of proper character who wished to undertake the task. He said that, if this last effort did not succeed, the government would be absolved of its responsibility for removal, which it had assumed at the urging of the citizens of Mississippi. The commissioner noted that some white people were actively encouraging the Choctaw to remain in the state, evidently speculators who still hoped to collect on their contracts for Choctaw lands.[64]

The continuing failure to effect the total removal of the Choctaw led the government finally to terminate all claims with a distribution of the money that had been allocated in lieu of scrip. The distribution of the money was made on the basis of a final census of the Choctaw in Mississippi, which was compiled in 1853 by Douglas Cooper, the special Indian agent. Cooper's roll listed 2,262 Choctaw. These included 193 in Louisiana; 514 of the Six Towns clan and 294 of the Chunka clan in Newton and Jasper counties; 359 of the Moglusha clan in Newton and Neshoba counties; 269 of the York nuk ne clan in Carrol and Leake counties; 69 of the Pearl River clan near that river; 403 of the Bogue Chitto clan in Neshoba County; 49 of the Haloon Iowah clan near Pearl River in Neshoba and Leake counties; 19 of the Sukanache clan in Kemper County; 63 of the Talla chulak clan in Kemper County; 16 of the Tush ka la meta clan in Scott County; and 13 of the Labatche clan in Leake and Neshoba counties.[65]

Cooper filed a final report with George Manypenny, commissioner of Indian affairs, on July 26, 1856. According to Cooper, the Choctaw denied that they had received a large portion of the scrip paid out by special agent Bowman in 1851. Since the scrip represented only half of what they were entitled to, many who did not want to move did not claim the scrip. The Choctaw acknowledged the receipt of some money. Cooper concluded that the Choctaw had agreed to pay to agents one-half of all the money they realized from their land claims under the Treaty of Dancing Rabbit Creek and that they had come forward to claim the scrip only because money was offered to them. He also claimed that Bowman had not reimbursed claimants for lost scrip. Cooper remarked:

> The Indians East, if let alone, would never think of claiming their scrip, which they admit belonged to their attornies and was received by some member of their respective families. They still to a great extent maintain their old tribal customs and usages, holding every thing belonging to a clan or *Iksa* in common. So if a member of the family gets what is due any portion of it they are satisfied.[66]

Cooper implied that Bowman was not entirely honest in his distribution of scrip, but no evidence is available to support the allegation.

With that final roll and payment of the money which had been appropriated by Congress to replace scrip, the last of the land claims were disposed of. Except for those few Choctaw who had received land patents based on Ward's register, and some who had received patents based on the 1838 commission report, the Choctaw were finally dispossessed.

The Treaty of Dancing Rabbit Creek and subsequent legislation affecting Choctaw claims in Mississippi reduced the Indians to a landless state, forcing them to live as squatters on public or private land, while the ceded land and the scrip for public land passed into the hands of land speculators. Although some of the Choctaw at the urging of speculators probably filed claims to land on which they had not actually lived, many doubtless had legitimate claims. Beginning with the actions of William Ward, the government had systematically deprived them of their rights. Ironically, much of the dispossession was disguised as concern to protect the Indians from land speculators who would have benefited if the land had been given to the Choctaw.

The Choctaw who remained in Mississippi were generally the most

Choctaw Land and Identity, 1830–1919

traditional members of the tribe. The institutions of their culture had been severely disrupted by the removal of the majority of the tribe. Clans and moieties could no longer function to regulate social relationships. The churches and schools that had been built among them by missionaries had ceased to exist when the missionaries moved west with their parishioners and pupils.

The Choctaw still had their language, of course, and some Indians were able to read and write it. Literacy in Choctaw resulted from the labors of missionaries such as Cyrus Byington, who translated the Bible and hymns into Choctaw as part of the effort to convert tribal members to Christianity. The translations nevertheless did much to preserve knowledge of the language.

Choctaw whose original claims had been entered by Ward, and some of those who had been specially named in the Treaty of Dancing Rabbit Creek, had land but were relatively few in number. Most Choctaw became squatters on unoccupied land of poor quality, often within the borders of swamps. They lived together in small communities and built their cabins as they had always done. They used wild foods, but they also planted small stands of corn, pumpkins, and potatoes. They had flocks of chickens and sometimes hogs. Hunting was still the most important part of their life-style.[67]

The stickball game remained an important part of Choctaw life, with its associated social activities and betting. Often as many as fifty players on each side would gather for the game. Also important were funeral customs. After burial of the deceased, the grave was marked with a pole and hoops. People mourned over the grave for a time after the death.[68]

The Choctaw occupied an anomalous position in the social structure of the antebellum South. They were not slaves, not landowners, not white, and not black. They did not fit into any of the accepted social and cultural classes of the time. They engaged in part-time wage labor as cotton pickers. They lived in fairly scattered locations and maintained social ties by traveling to ball games or dances to visit and exchange news. Singing and dancing were major social activities. Traditional beliefs in spirits of nature, ghosts, and witches were strong, and traditional healing practices and knowledge of herbal medicines continued.[69]

The distinctive Choctaw identity both enforced and was reinforced

Clara Sue Kidwell

Choctaw dances performed impromptu in the tribal office parking lot during the Choctaw Fair. *Photo: William Brescia*

by the social isolation of their lives. They persisted as a separate group, held together by language and customs, but without any land base or political institutions. They lived by marginal farming, hunting, and occasional wage labor. The greatest change in their lives before the late 1870s resulted from Reconstruction. With the freeing of the slaves and the development of the institution of sharecropping, the main social distinction between Indians and blacks disappeared. Neither was free, and both became tenant farmers or sharecroppers working on the farms of white landowners.[70]

The change to sharecropping as a way of life probably came later for the Choctaw than for the blacks. When the rich delta area of Mississippi became more attractive to white and black farmers, many moved away from the poorer land in central Mississippi, and the Choctaw became more desirable as tenants. By 1900 most lived as sharecroppers in small, stable communities. The sharecropping system tended, however, to perpetuate the same kind of dependency that had been their lot since the Europeans introduced trade among them. As sharecroppers they became indebted to the landlords, and their produce paid their debts.[71]

The major white institution that had become important to the Choctaw before the removal period was the mission school. The missionaries, however, moved west with their native parishioners. Not until the late 1870s did Christian missions begin again to affect Choctaw life, but their impact was to be important.

In about 1878 a Baptist church was organized by a group of blacks near Carthage, Mississippi, and some Choctaw began to attend, despite their rather strong prejudice against blacks. A request was then sent to the Mississippi Baptist Association for an Indian missionary. The request was forwarded to the Oklahoma Baptist Church, and in 1879 Peter Folsom was sent from Oklahoma to Mississippi, where he established a church. He was assisted by Jesse Baker, a Mississippi Choctaw who taught reading and writing in Choctaw. Baker eventually replaced Folsom, who returned to Oklahoma in 1881. Baker died shortly thereafter, and another Oklahoma missionary, James Brown, was sent. Brown was ill when he arrived and he died almost immediately. Despite these calamities, the Choctaw organized the Hopewell Baptist Church in 1885.[72]

The Baptist church became a new source of social activity and leadership among the Choctaw. It also precipitated divisions within communities. Some Indians perpetuated the traditional social activities, such as dances and stickball games (with the drinking and gambling that usually accompanied them); the church members frowned on this recreation. In some way, being a traditional Choctaw seemed antithetical to being a Baptist Choctaw. Still, the churches became places where communities could gather despite any doctrinal differences.

The Baptist church succeeded among the Choctaw partly because it was basically democratic in nature. The church was run by native preachers, and each church was virtually autonomous. The people thus controlled the institution, and it was not subject to outside influences.[73]

The church was also a source of social contact that bore similarities to traditional customs. Men and women sat on opposite sides of the building, and after the service, dinner was generally served on the lawn. During the dinner the men and women either ate separately or sat facing each other at long tables. Sometimes ball games would be held in the afternoon.[74]

Despite the very basic difference in beliefs between the Baptist Choctaw and the traditional Choctaw, the church nevertheless retained the support of the community because it was controlled by the people themselves, and its language was that of the people. By 1891, when the Choctaw in Mississippi numbered 2,000 people, there were nine Baptist churches with eight ministers and approximately 300 members.[75] Methodist missionaries also established four churches among the Choctaw in 1898–1899, but the influence of the Methodists remained slight, and only one church still existed by 1903.[76]

Catholicism became an influence in the winter of 1883–1884, when a Belgian priest, Father Bekkers, established a mission near the community of Tucker and attempted to persuade the Choctaw to move into an area around the mission where he had purchased land. In 1898 a Catholic church was built, and by 1900 it had a membership of 690 Indians and 108 whites. The church acquired 1,400 acres and encouraged Choctaw families to settle there, thus creating the nexus of a Choctaw community.[77]

One of the most important contributions of the Catholic missionaries was the establishment of a school for Choctaw children in conjunction with the mission. The first teacher at the school was Henry Sales Halbert, whose reports about the Mississippi Choctaw schools are an important source of information about the tribe.[78] By 1882 the Mississippi legislature had passed "An Act to establish public schools for the Indians in East Mississippi."[79] By the 1892–1893 school year, five Choctaw schools were in operation in Mississippi with an all-white teaching staff and 126 children enrolled. Halbert acted as the state's overseer of these schools. The school year was eighty days (sixty days for one school), and 20 students attended public school in Jasper County.[80]

Halbert mentioned some of the problems confronting Choctaw schools:

> The poverty of the Indians is the great cause of much irregular attendance of some of the children. Their parents frequently need their services at home

in labor upon the farm and otherwise. During the winter, in inclement weather, the want of sufficient clothing, especially with those children who live at a distance, not unfrequently cause an irregularity of attendance.

Halbert carried out instruction in Choctaw and English, pointing out that:

> Our native Mississippi Choctaws are strongly attached to their native tongue, and there is no immediate prospect of its being supplanted by English. Even those most proficient have, at last, only a superficial knowledge of the language, and great numbers of the children have none at all.[81]

He sometimes taught reading and writing in Choctaw to his pupils. During the period from 1891 to 1899, seven schools were operated at various times. Some were public and some were private. The school year was generally about eighty days long, and attendance was irregular. The teachers, however, praised the intelligence and quickness of their pupils.[82]

The schools not only served the children of the Choctaw communities but also became social centers for the adults. Traditional games such as chunky and stickball, as well as baseball, were played on the grounds, and men met regularly to discuss problems. Schoolteachers did not approve of these activities.[83] Community life thus came to center on the church and the school (in the case of parochial schools the two were generally in the same building). Traditional activities such as ball games coexisted, although not always happily, with schools and religious services.

Education seems to have had little impact on the community of Bogue Chitto, whose residents, according to Halbert, were "the most barbarous and non-progressive of all our Choctaws."[84] The explanation given for their resistance was that schools had been established before the signing of the Treaty of Dancing Rabbit Creek, and the Bogue Chitto Choctaw feared that new schools would herald yet another forced migration.[85]

The Dawes act, also known as the General Allotment Act, passed in 1887 and posed a threat to the Choctaw communities in Mississippi. Although it did not affect the tribes in the Indian Territory, it set the stage for the division of Indian lands into individual holdings, with the breakup of tribal reservations. Allotment was finally imposed upon the

Choctaw, Chickasaw, Creeks, and Seminole in the Indian Territory by the Curtis act, passed in June 1898.[86]

The Choctaw in the Indian Territory became interested in the situation of the Mississippi Choctaw, and they asked Congress to provide money for removal to the West in Oklahoma.[87] Although Congress did not act, many Choctaw from Mississippi moved west of their own accord. The Choctaw Tribal Council in Indian Territory passed several acts to grant citizenship to the newcomers, and in 1891 it appropriated $1,792.50 to pay the expenses of removal and provided for the appointment of two commissioners to go to Mississippi, to collect the Choctaw there, and to escort them to Indian Territory.[88]

An act of Congress on June 7, 1898, made it the duty of the Commission to the Five Civilized Tribes (also known as the Dawes commission, which had been appointed to allot the land of the Five Civilized Tribes in Oklahoma) to report to Congress whether the Mississippi Choctaw would have to take up residence in the Choctaw Nation and to remain in residence for three years before they could receive allotments.[89]

Early in 1900 representatives of the Dawes commission traveled to Mississippi and compiled a roll of 2,335 Choctaw. Because of cold weather, the fact that the commission stopped at relatively few places, and the resistance of certain groups (notably the Bogue Chitto) to the work of the commission, about 500 were not enrolled.[90]

As had occurred after the Treaty of Dancing Rabbit Creek, some people wanted to take advantage of the Choctaw. Some came forward to say that they would help the Choctaw establish their claims to land in Oklahoma in exchange for half the value of the lands to be received. Agents circulated in the towns and placed advertisements in newspapers throughout the Southeast. A number of claims of supposed Choctaw were brought forward by lawyers for the claimants. The majority of these claims were ultimately denied by the government.[91]

In 1903 Congress appropriated money to aid the removal of the full-blood Mississippi Choctaw, and before the year was over, about 300 of them had been brought by train to the Indian Territory. Others were moved by land speculators who hoped to gain title to the allotments.[92]

The social and community life that had evolved around the churches and schools in Mississippi was disrupted by this second removal as the old traditions and institutions had been during the first removal. Most of the workers at the Catholic mission in Tucker moved to Oklahoma. Only one Methodist church remained by 1903, and the Baptist churches had been moving rather steadily to the West even before the removal of 1903. The schools were abandoned by the state in 1900, probably in anticipation of removal.[93]

Again, however, the removal was not complete, and the more traditional people, particularly those who had resisted enrollment by the Dawes commission, remained behind. The core identity, language, and customs remained with them. Many also remained Christian, attending the Catholic mission and several Baptist churches. By 1911 the Choctaw Baptist churches had formed the New Choctaw Baptist Association, breaking away from the white Baptist church.[94]

Sharecropping continued as the primary way of life, with women's basketmaking supplementing family income. Culture and race still placed the Mississippi Choctaw outside the social and political structure of the South. They retained their strong prejudice against blacks. They generally chose not to mix with either white or black elements of the Mississippi population.[95]

In 1910 the Mississippi Choctaw population was 1,253, according to the U.S. census. The decline in population from the 2,335 enrolled by the Dawes commission in 1903, however, represented at least a 50 percent loss of population. Although some of the Choctaws who had moved to the Indian Territory eventually returned to Mississippi, the population decline remained drastic. The stability of the communities was further disrupted by a great influenza epidemic. The 1920 census showed a decline in population among the Choctaw of 148 from the 1910 count.[96]

The situation of the Mississippi Choctaw came to the attention of Congress as a result of the attempts at removal and the continuing efforts to open the Choctaw citizenship rolls in the new state of Oklahoma. Even after the Dawes commission had left Mississippi for Oklahoma, people continued to come forward with claims to rights in Oklahoma.[97]

Congress conducted a series of hearings in 1917 to determine the condition of the Choctaw and their needs for additional land and school facilities. The testimony of the Choctaw indicated to the commissioners that most lived in very poor conditions, primarily as sharecroppers.

Some Indians reported, however, that their children went to school, and some said that they themselves knew how to read and write Choctaw and that their children were learning to do so. The commissioners also learned that most of the Choctaw lived on very small incomes in small cabins with poor ventilation.[98]

John R. T. Reeves, a special supervisor for the Indian Service, filed a report on the investigations in 1916. He noted that the Indian children were not allowed to attend white schools and that they refused to attend schools for black children. Neshoba and Leake counties had provided separate schools for Indian children, but other counties had not done so. In Leake County, from a total of 95 Indian children of school age, 45 were enrolled in two schools. In Neshoba County, with 254 Indian children of school age, the aggregate enrollment in three Indian schools was 40.[99]

Reeves summarized the situation:

> The schools maintained by the State are of the most elementary character and remain in session for a few months only of each year, frequently not over four or five. The total expense of conducting the six Indian schools during the past session . . . was $566. But little more could really be expected of the State, as only a few of the Indians are property owners and taxpayers.[100]

When Indians owned land, it was heavily mortgaged. Reeves investigated forty-one Indian land holdings, most of them consisting of eighty acres of less. He noted that a severe tropical storm during the preceding year had destroyed much of the corn and cotton crops, causing severe hardship to non-Indian as well as Indian farmers.

> The land owned by the Indians is of the most inferior quality . . . usually this is heavily encumbered. Again, it should be borne in mind that less than 10 per cent of the Indians are assessed with any property at all. The vast majority of them own nothing and are practically destitute, living in decrepit shacks and cabins that but indifferently afford protection against the elements.[101]

The main source of income for most of the Indians, according to Reeves, was not sharecropping but wage labor such as cotton picking or woodcutting. Reeves's report concluded by recommending that a boardingschool be established in the Indians' midst and that a limited quantity of land be set aside per individual. The most pressing need, however, was "not so much for additional land as . . . for relief in the form of clothing and subsistence to keep many of these Indians from great suffering if not actual starvation."[102]

Congress subsequently passed a bill granting the Mississippi Choctaw de facto recognition as an Indian tribe. An agency was created for them in 1918. The purchase of land was authorized, and small reservations were created around the Choctaw communities. The Choctaw were thus restored to their status before the Treaty of Dancing Rabbit Creek, at least to the extent that they were now a federally recognized Indian tribe. Their land, a part of that ceded by Treaty of Dancing Rabbit Creek, was held in trust for them by the federal government. Still, the Choctaw had regained a very small fraction of what they had given up in 1830. The formation of government commissions had resulted in such delays that people who had been deprived of land by Agent William Ward could probably never have their claims legitimately settled. The people who wished to remain in Mississippi because it was their homeland and the source of their culture did so in spite of, rather than because of, the actions of the U.S. government. They retained both their customs and their language. Although they lived in poverty, and in many instances had to work for white settlers as sharecroppers, they managed to preserve their identity as Choctaw.

Notes

1. Charles J. Kappler, *Indian Affairs: Laws and Treaties* (Washington, D.C.: Government Printing Office, 1904–29), 2: 313–14.
2. *Land Claims Etc. under the Fourteenth Article*, 24th Cong., 1st sess., May 11, 1836, H. Rept. 663, pp. 41–47.
3. Ibid., 18–20.
4. Ibid., 32–33, 41–47.
5. *Report from the Secretary of the Treasury*, 24th Cong., 1st sess., January 20, 1836, S. Doc. 69, pp. 4–5.
6. *In Relation to the Location of Reservations . . .*, 23rd Cong., 1st sess., April 11, 1834, S. Rept. 1230; *American State Papers: Public Lands*, 7: 1–139.
7. George W. Martin to Lewis Cass, September 15, 1833, in *Choctaw Nation of Indians v. United States*, U.S. Court of Claims No. 12742, at 38–39; John M. Moore to Elbert Herring, June 17, 1833, 24th Cong., 1st sess., S. Rept. 69, 3.
8. Martin to Cass, September 11, 1833, *Choctaw Nation v. United States* at 37.
9. Ibid., September 15, 1833, at 38.
10. Ibid., August 9, 1833, at 36–37; ibid., September 11, 1833, at 37.
11. Ibid., December 6, 1833, at 42–43.
12. Mahlon Dickerson to Martin, October 13, 1834, in ibid. at 34.
13. *Choctaw Nation v. United States* at 54.
14. Martin to Cass, August 20, 1834, in ibid., at 44.
15. Ibid., December 29, 1834, at 52.

16. Affidavit of Grabel Lincecum, Lowndes County, December 22, 1834, *Choctaw Removal Records*, Record Group 75, National Archives (hereafter cited as RG 75, NA), Entry 268; *Choctaw Nation v. United States* at 56.
17. *Land Claims etc. under the Fourteenth Article*, 24th Cong., 1st sess., May 11, 1836, H. Rept. 663, pp. 41–47.
18. W. Ward to Saml. S. Hamilton, June 31, 1831, *Choctaw Nation v. United States* at 17.
19. *Choctaw Indians*, 24th Cong., 1st sess., February 1, 1836, H. Doc. 119, pp. 1–3.
20. *Indian Claims in Mississippi, Petition of the Citizens of the State of Mississippi, Remonstrating against Indian Claims*, 24th Cong., 1st sess., February 1, 1836, H. Doc., 89, pp. 1–2.
21. John H. Peterson, Jr., "The Mississippi Band of Choctaw Indians: Their Recent History and Current Social Relations" (Ph.D. diss., University of Georgia, 1970), pp. 15–16.
22. *In The Senate of the United States*, 24th Cong., 1st sess., March 22, 1836, S. Doc. 265, pp. 5–6.
23. *Message from the President*, 25th Cong., 2d sess., December 19, 1837, S. Doc. 25, p. 2.
24. *U.S. Statutes at Large* (Washington, D.C.: Government Printing Office, 1852), 5:180 (hereafter cited as 5 *Stat. L.*).
25. *Message from the President*, 25th Cong., 2d sess., December 19, 1837, S. Doc. 25, pp. 3–4, 21, 23.
26. P. D. Vroom, J. Murray, Roger Barton to C. A. Harris, March 1, 1838, *Choctaw Nation v. United States* at 126.
27. 5 *Stat. L.*, 211.
28. RG 75, NA, Entry 268, pp. 115–32; *Choctaw Nation v. United States* at 150–214.
29. *Choctaw Nation v. United States* at 135.
30. Murray and P. D. Vroom to the President, July 31, 1838, in ibid. at 131–36.
31. *Reservations of Land under Fourteenth Article of Treaty of 1830 with the Choctaw Indians*, 25th Cong., 3d sess., H. Rep. 294.
32. Murray and Vroom to President, July 31, 1838, *Choctaw Nation v. United States* at 134.
33. *Letter from the Secretary of War in Relation to the Adjustment of Claims Arising under the Fourteenth and Nineteenth Articles*, 27th Cong., 2d sess., March 16, 1842, S. Doc. 188, p.2.
34. *Message from the President . . . in Relation to the Proceedings and Conduct of the Choctaw Commission . . .*, 28th cong., 1st sess., January 30, 1844, S. Doc. 168; 5 *Stat. L.*, 513.
35. 5 *Stat. L.*, 513–16.
36. *Message from the President*, S. Doc. 168; Hartley Crawford to Claiborne, Graves, and Barton, October 24, 1842, in ibid., 10.
37. Kirksey and Poindexter to Graves and Claiborn, January 16, 1843, in *Message from the President*, S. Doc. 168, pp. 18–19.
38. Charles Fisher to Commissioners, undated, in *Message from the President*, S. Doc. 168, p. 21.
39. RG 75, NA, Entry 268; Charles Fisher Papers, folder 43, drafts of power of attorney, assignment of claims, Southern History Collection, University of North Carolina, Chapel Hill.
40. Tyler and Graves to T. Hartley Crawford, April 15, 1843, in *Message from the President*, S. Doc 168, p. 29–30.
41. Crawford to J. C. Spencer, in *Message from the President*, S. Doc. 168.
42. R. J. Walker to President John Tyler, May 10, 1843, in *Message from the President*,

S. Doc. 168, pp. 41–42; Reuben Grant to Commission of Indian Affairs, June 3, 1843, in ibid., 57.

43. Report by Commissioner Graves, RG 75, NA, Entry 275.

44. Suggestions by Claiborne, May 109, 1843, in *Message from the President*, S. Doc. 168, pp. 51–54; Graves to Crawford, June 10, 1843, ibid., 80–81.

45. T. J. Word to Board of Commissioners, August 16, 1843, in *Message from the President*, S. Doc. 168, pp. 107–18.

46. Statement by John F. H. Claiborne, May 10, 1843, in *Message from the President*, S. Doc. 168, pp. 53–55.

47. John A. Freeman to J. F. H. Claiborne, November 21, 1842, Claiborne Papers, Library of Congress; Mary Elizabeth Young, *Redskins, Ruffleshirts, and Rednecks: Allotments in Alabama and Mississippi, 1830–1860* (Norman: University of Oklahoma Press, 1961), 63.

48. Secretary of War Report . . . *Removal and Subsistence of the Choctaw Indian*, 28th Cong., 2d sess., February 17, 1845, S. Doc. 86, p. 32.

49. John McRae to Crawford, February 6, 1843, Office of Indian Affairs, Letters Received, microfilm M-234 (hereaster cited as OIA, LR, M-234), roll 185, RG 75, NA.

50. McRae to Crawford, February 18, 1843, OIA, LR, M-234.

51. John F. H. Claiborne, *Memorial*, 28th Cong., 1st sess., February 19, 1844, H. Doc. 137, pp. 1–2, 5.

52. Ibid.

53. Ibid., 183–85; Secretary of War *Letter . . . Fourteenth and Nineteenth Articles*, 27th Cong., 2d sess., March 16, 1842, S. Doc. 188, pp. 183–85.

54. U.S. Court of Claims, /12742, Choctaw Nation vs. U.S., Evidence, pp. 494–95.

55. *Choctaw Treaty*, 29th Cong., 1st sess., April 27, 1846, H. Doc. 189, p. 2; RG 75, NA, Entry 279, Choctaw Claims Under the 14th Article of the Treaty of 1830. Revision of the Decisions of Messrs. Claiborne, Graves and Tyler.

56. February 7, 1845, S. Doc. 86, 28th Cong., 2d Sess., p. 13. Report of the Secretary of War—Information in Relation to the Contracts Made for the Removal and Subsistence of the Choctaw Indians.

57. John R. Swanton, *Source Material for the Social and Ceremonial Life of the Choctaw Indians*, Bureau of American Ethnology, Bulletin No. 103 (Washington, D.C.: Government Printing office, 1931), 5.

58. 5 *Stat. L.*, 777.

59. Henry L. Scott to Orlando Brown, November 17, 1849, OIA, LR, M-234, roll 187, RG 75, NA.

60. S. Easterling to Secretary of War, August 4, 1847, OIA, LR, M-234, roll 187, RG 75, NA.

61. Commissioner of Indian Affairs, *Report*, 29th Cong., 1st sess., November 30, 1845, S. Exec. Doc. 1, p. 448.

62. Commissioner of Indian Affairs, *Report*, 29th Cong. 2d sess., November 30, 1846, S. Exec. Doc. 1, p. 214.

63. Commissioner of Indian Affairs, *Report*, 30th Cong., 1st sess., November 30, 1847, S. Exec. Doc. 1, p. 735.

64. Commissioner of Indian Affairs, *Report*, 30th Cong., 2d sess., November 30, 1848, S. Exec. Doc. 1.

65. General Roll of Choctaw Families Residing East of the Mississippi . . . , dated May 23, 1855, RG 75, NA, Entry 267.

66. Ibid.

67. Peterson, "Mississippi Band of Choctaw Indians," 29; Peterson, "Louisiana Choctaw Life at the End of the Eighteenth Century," in *Four Centuries of Southern Indians*, ed. Charles Hudson (Athens: University of Georgia Press, 1975), 106. Although these

descriptions are based on accounts of Louisiana Choctaw villages in the late 1800s, when the people had more contact with white settlers, some of the Mississippi Choctaw probably lived in similar situations.

68. A. J. Brown, *History of Newton County, Mississippi, from 1834 to 1894* (Jackson: Clarion-Ledger, 1894), 15–16; J. F. H. Claiborne, *Mississippi as a Province, Territory, and State* (Jackson: Power and Barksdale, 1880), 1:489.

69. David I. Bushnell, Jr., *The Choctaw of Bayou Lacombe, St. Tamany Parish, Louisiana*, Smithsonian Institution, Bureau of American Ethnology, Bulletin No. 48 (Washington, D.C.: Government Printing Office, 1909), 23–24, 28–29; Brown, *History of Newton County*, 16–17.

70. Peterson, "The Mississippi Band of Choctaw Indians," 50.

71. Peterson, "The Mississippi Band of Choctaw Indians," 56–58; Mississippi Band of Choctaw Indians, "Overall Economic Development Program, 1978–1982" (Philadelphia, Miss., 1977), 15.

72. Peterson, "The Mississippi Band of Choctaw Indians," 64–66; Eugene I. Farr, "Religious Assimilation: A Case Study of the Adoption of Christianity by the Choctaw Indians of Mississippi" (Th.D. diss., New Orleans Baptist Theological Seminary, 1948).

73. Charles Madden Tolbert, "A Sociological Study of the Choctaw Indians in Mississippi" (Ph.D. diss., Louisiana State University, 1958), 220; Farr, "Religious Assimilation," 75; Brown, *History of Newton County*, 273.

74. Charles Mitchell Beckett, "Choctaw Indians in Mississippi since 1830" (master's thesis, Oklahoma Agricultural and Mechanical College, 1949), 63–64.

75. Farr, "Religious Assimilation," 32.

76. Ibid., 33.

77. Peterson, "The Mississippi Band of Choctaw Indians," 77; Reverend Richard O. Gerow, *Catholicity in Mississippi* (Natchez: Hope Haven Press, 1939), 263–64; G. E. Lindquist, *The Red Man in the United States: An Intimate Study of the Social, Economic, and Religious Life of the American Indian* (New York: Doran, 1923), 114.

78. H. S. Halbert, "Funeral Customs of the Mississippi Choctaws," *Publications of the Mississippi Historical Society* 3 (1903): 353n.

79. *Laws of the State of Mississippi Passed at a Regular Session of the Legislature . . . Commencing Jan. 3d, 1882 and Ending March 9, 1882* (Jackson: Power, 1882), 77.

80. Henry Sales Halbert, "Indian Schools in Mississippi," in *Biennial Report of the State Superintendent of Public Education to the Legislature of Mississippi for Scholastic Years 1891–92 and 1892–93* (Jackson: Clarion-Ledger, 1894), 574.

81. Ibid., 575.

82. Henry Sales Halbert, "The Mississippi Choctaws," in *Biennial Report . . . for Scholastic Years 1897–98 and 1898–99* (Jacksonville, Fla.: Lance, 1900), 35.

83. Henry Sales Halbert, "Indian Schools," in *Biennial Report . . . for Scholastic Years 1895–96 and 1896–97* (Jackson: Clarion-Ledger, 1898), 24.

84. Henry Sales Halbert, "The Indians in Mississippi and Their Schools," in *Biennial Report . . . for Scholastic Years 1893–94 and 1894–95* (Jackson: Clarion-Ledger, 1895), 536.

85. Ibid., 576; Halbert, "Indian Schools," 26; Halbert, "The Mississippi Choctaws," 36.

86. Angie Debo, *The Rise and Fall of the Choctaw Republic*, 2d ed. (Norman: University of Oklahoma Press, 1961), 262.

87. *Mississippi Choctaws*, 54th Cong., 2d sess., March 3, 1897, H. Doc. 3080, pp. 3–4.

88. Debo, *Choctaw Republic*, 181.

89. Commission to the Five Civilized Tribes, *A Report Relative to the Mississippi Choctaws*, 55th Cong., 2d sess., February 3, 1898, H. Rep. 274, pp. 2–5.

90. Commission to the Five Civilized Tribes, *Report to the Secretary of the Interior*

for the Year Ended June 30, 1905 (Washington, D.C.: Government Printing Office, 1905), 16, 92; Commission to the Five Civilized Tribes, *Eleventh Annual Report to the Secretary of the Interior for the Fiscal Year Ended June 30, 1904* (Washington, D.C.: Government Printing Office, 1904), 18–19.

91. U.S. Department of the Interior, *Report of Inspector James McLaughlin on Bills for Enrollment with the Five Civilized Tribes, July 2, 1914* (Washington, D.C.: Government Printing Office, 1916).

92. Debo, *Choctaw Republic*, 273–76.

93. Beckett, "Choctaw Indians," 36–37; Farr, "Religious Assimilation," 32–33; Peterson, "The Mississippi Band of Choctaw Indians," 89, 97.

94. Farr, "Religious Assimilation," 70–71.

95. Halbert, "The Mississippi Choctaws," 109; Farr, "Religious Assimilation," 19; Tolbert, "A Sociological Study," 125–26; H. Kirkland Osoinach, "The Dynamics of Mississippi Choctaw Society: An Exploratory Formulation" (University of Chicago, Department of Anthropology, 1960), 31.

96. Peterson, "The Mississippi Band of Choctaw Indians," 109; Mississippi Band of Choctaw Indians, "Overall Economic Development Plan," 17.

97. William Sydney Coker, "Pat Harrison's Efforts to Reopen the Choctaw Citizenship Rolls," *Southern Quarterly* 3 (October 1964): 49–59.

98. U.S. Congress, House, Committee on Investigation of the Indian Service, *Condition of the Mississippi Choctaws, Hearings*, vol. 2: (Washington, D.C.: Government Printing Office, 1917), pp. 150–53.

99. John Reeves, *Additional Land and Indian Schools in Mississippi*, 64th Cong., 2d sess., March 16, 1917, H. Doc. 1464, pp. 2, 6, 11.

100. Ibid., 14.

101. Ibid., 24.

102. Ibid., 28.

6

The Second Choctaw Removal, 1903

Charles Roberts

In the summer and fall of 1903, the federal government transported 290 Mississippi and Louisiana Choctaw to the Choctaw Nation in the Indian Territory.[1] This removal was part of a larger relocation that took as many as 1,462 Choctaw to the West by March 4, 1907, when tribal rolls were closed. Of the 2,534 Mississippi Choctaw identified in the annual report of the commissioner of Indian affairs for 1907, 1,072 had chosen to stay in Mississippi or were not given notice sufficient to permit them to make a decision.[2] This removal was instigated by the government's decision to terminate the existence of the Choctaw Nation and to divide its resources among all members of the tribe, in keeping with the Curtis act of 1898. By the terms of Article 14 of the treaty of 1830, which were subsequently confirmed by the treaty of 1866, Mississippi Choctaw were eligible to share in the distribution of land if they left Mississippi and made settlement in the Choctaw or Chickasaw nations. Their departure, however, had serious consequences for them and for the communities they left behind.[3]

For Mississippi Choctaw the two decades prior to the removal of 1903 were an era of significant social and economic change. After the first removal of the 1830s and 1840s, they had retreated into the marginal areas of their homeland. Their isolation enabled them to survive in a society that defined itself in black and white. As long as slavery existed, the racial mores of Mississippi did not recognize people who were not black slaves or white citizens. After the Civil War, however, new possibilities opened up. Foremost among these was sharecropping. With a greater degree of mobility now possible, many of the freedmen migrated to the richer lands of the Yazoo delta, creating a labor shortage in the areas they left behind. As the woods were clear-cut, more land was opened for farming and attracted an influx of white people. Some of the Choctaw found jobs in the lumber industry, but for most it became increasingly necessary to make sharecropping arrangements with local white farmers. Under these circumstances, the Choctaw could no longer remain insulated from the wider currents of American life.[4]

An important change for the Choctaw was the renewal of Christian missionary work. In 1880, Peter Folsom, a seventy-seven-year-old Oklahoma Choctaw, was invited to conduct mission work among the Mississippi Choctaw. Folsom, an ordained Baptist minister, was born in Mississippi and had been removed to the Indian Territory in the 1830s. He established the Mount Zion Baptist Church, the first among the Mississippi Choctaw since removal. His efforts inspired a series of visits by the Oklahoma Choctaw and the development of a native Mississippi Choctaw ministry. By 1892 there were nine Choctaw Baptist churches in Mississippi, with eight ordained ministers and an aggregate membership of 393. They included Macedonia near Conehatta in Newton County and Bethany near Philadelphia in Neshoba County, both established in 1890. There were also four Methodist churches. The first of these was Black Jack in Neshoba County, established by Simson Tubby. Tubby was the first Mississippi Choctaw since the 1830s to attend college. He matriculated at Millsaps College in Jackson, Mississippi, in preparation for mission work. Other Methodist churches were established at Talla Chula in Kemper County and at Conehatta.[5]

Perhaps the most significant mission work was conducted by the Catholic church. In 1880 the Right Reverend Bishop Francis Janssen of Natchez, Mississippi, paid a visit to Neshoba County and noticed the condition of the Choctaw. Two years later, during a visit to Holland, he approached Father B. J. Bekkers and suggested that he begin mission work in Mississippi. Bekkers agreed and set sail for the United States. He established himself in Neshoba County and by September 1884 had purchased 480 acres at Tucker, seven miles southeast of Philadelphia, where he constructed a number of log cabins. He established Holy Rosary Church and invited the local Choctaw to reside at the mission and to work the land. Tom Billy was the first to accept. On a trip to Holland in 1887, Bekkers raised a sum of $5,420, which he used to purchase an additional 1,400 acres at Tucker. Bekkers placed a high value on education. In 1884, he opened a school for the Choctaw and hired H. S. Halbert to be its teacher. In its first year the school had twenty-six pupils. On September 30, 1885, three Sisters of Mercy from Vicksburg joined the mission staff and assumed responsibility for teaching at the school and for adult education. Halbert was released, but he remained closely associated with Choctaw education for the rest of his career. By 1890 the mission at Tucker had 242 Choctaw and 58 whites as members. By 1900 this number had increased to 690 Choctaw and 108 whites, a significant proportion of the Choctaw population. In 1898 Bekkers retired and accepted an assignment in Meridian, Mississippi. He was replaced the next year by three Carmelite Fathers and three lay Brothers.[6]

The state of Mississippi also took an interest in Choctaw education. In the early 1890s the state government began to support schools in the various Choctaw communities. H. S. Halbert, who was appointed director of this system, reported that for the school year 1892–1893 there were five Choctaw schools with an enrollment of 126 students. By October 1895, Halbert reported that all of the Choctaw communities, with the exception of Pearl River and Bogue Chitto, had acquired teachers and school buildings. In the two communities that continued to lack schools, and especially at Bogue Chitto, many Choctaw feared that education would ultimately bring removal to the Indian Territory. In this regard their fears seem to have been prophetic.[7]

In the last decade of the nineteenth century, efforts were repeatedly made to persuade Mississippi Choctaw to emigrate west to the Indian Territory. On December 24, 1889, the Oklahoma Choctaw passed a resolution, urging the federal government to appropriate sufficient funds to assist any Choctaw who were willing to be removed to the Choctaw Nation. Congress refused, however, to approve such legislation at that time. The Choctaw National Council nevertheless appropriated $1,792.50 of its own funds on October 20, 1891, and charged James S. Standley, a mixed-blood Choctaw who had emigrated to the Choctaw Nation from Mississippi in 1873, with the task of bringing Mississippi Choctaw west to join their kinsmen. Standley, who had risen to

The Second Choctaw Removal, 1903

prominence as a Choctaw delegate to Washington, D.C., and as editor of the *Indian Citizen* of Atoka, successfully recruited 124 Mississippi Choctaw. Prior to 1895, smaller groups of Mississippi Choctaw were also persuaded to remove to the Indian Territory.[8]

In 1893 the U.S. Congress established the Special Commission to the Five Civilized Tribes, known as the Dawes commission after its first chairman, Henry F. Dawes, a senator from Massachusetts who had recently retired. The Dawes commission was authorized to conduct negotiations that resulted in the dissolution of the tribal governments of Indian Territory and the allotment of land to the individual members of the tribes. In 1897 the commission was ordered by Congress to ascertain the eligibility of Mississippi and Louisiana Choctaw to share in this distribution of land. The commission reported that these Indians would be eligible if they established residence in the Choctaw or Chickasaw nations and if they could establish their identities under Article 14 of the treaty of 1830. In 1898 the Curtis act made it the duty of the commission to compile a roll of eligible Choctaw, including those who lived in Mississippi. A. S. McKennon, a member of the commission, established headquarters in Meridian in January 1899. During the next few months he identified 2,240 Mississippi Choctaw, although he probably overlooked as many as 400 Choctaw who were suspicious of the government's purposes and refused to be interviewed. The overwhelming number of these Choctaw could not prove descent from ancestors who had applied for reservations of land at the time of removal. Only ten Mississippi Choctaw were able to provide documents that proved their eligibility. It was clear to the commission, however, that most of the Choctaw were full-bloods and could be assumed to have descended from Choctaw who had not been removed in the 1830s and 1840s.[9]

Between April 1, 1901, and April 30, 1902, members of the Dawes commission returned to Mississippi and conducted an intensive investigation to identify full-blood Mississippi Choctaw. A field party left Meridian on October 11, 1901, and returned on January 13, 1902. A second trip was made on February 17, 1902, and returned to Meridian on April 13. The commission reported that 2,534 full-blood Choctaw had been identified and were eligible for allotments in the Choctaw and Chickasaw nations. Consequently, the problem of determining eligibility for allotments was resolved in the supplementary agreement of July 1, 1902, which simply asserted that full-bloods were eligible for removal and for their share in the distribution of land. Mixed-bloods, however, would still have to prove their ancestry.[10]

Since few of the Mississippi Choctaw could pay their own expenses in emigrating west, a large number of speculators stepped into the breach, offering financial assistance for liens upon the allotments that the Choctaw would receive. The speculators claimed to control the best land in the Indian Territory and said they would pay for transportation and for the cost of settlement. Prior to the passage of the supplementary agreement, they concentrated on mixed-blood Choctaw or on anyone who claimed to be a Choctaw. Applications poured in from all parts of the country. Robert L. Owen, a mixed-blood Cherokee and a former Union agent, together with his associate, Charles F. Wilson, signed hundreds of these contracts, and their claims were eventually upheld. In 1922 they were awarded $175,000 to be paid from Mississippi Choctaw per capita funds.[11] The large number of claimants overwhelmed the Dawes commission as it sought to determine eligibility, and a special Choctaw-Chickasaw Citizenship Court was created. By the time the rolls had been closed in 1907, this court and the commission had rejected 22,150 applications from persons who claimed to be Mississippi Choctaw. After the agreement went into effect, speculators focused on the full-blood population.[12]

The federal government, now painfully aware of the venality of the speculators as well as of the impoverished state of most Mississippi Choctaw, decided to intervene. On March 3, 1903, Congress established a fund of $20,000 to be expended by the Dawes commission for the removal of all identified and indigent Mississippi and Louisiana Choctaw.[13] On July 2, 1903, E. A. Hitchcock, the secretary of the interior, wrote to the commission, authorizing it to proceed in removing Mississippi Choctaw and averring that, "owing to the limited time provided for in section 41 of the Act of Congress of July 1, 1902," it was necessary that the work "be entered into at once and carried to completion with as little delay as possible."[14] Because its members were on vacation, the commission was slow to act. Not until July 24 was H. Van V. Smith of Muskogee, Indian Territory, ordered to report to Meridian and to persuade the Choctaw to emigrate. Of the full-bloods, 700 had to be removed by August 14 if they were to share in allotments of land.[15]

The Second Choctaw Removal, 1903

Smith arrived in Meridian on July 27 and set up headquarters on the second floor of the federal building. He immediately issued a "Special Notice to Full-Blood Mississippi Choctaws," dated July 27, 1903, and posted throughout central and northeastern Mississippi. This circular declared that Smith had been authorized by the secretary of the interior to remove Mississippi Choctaw and that he required them to "call on me or write to me immediately" so that he could at once "investigate their condition and provide free transportation and free rations as their status and circumstances may justify and require." On the same day Smith sent individual letters to all Choctaw previously identified by the Dawes commission. Each of the letters stated that the recipient had been identified as a full-blood Mississippi Choctaw and that the six months required by law for removal were to expire on Friday, August 14. Smith encouraged each person to report to Meridian by the afternoon of August 11 for the journey to the Indian Territory by special train on August 12.[16]

Smith also hired "five competent men, who are thoroughly familiar with leading full-blood Choctaws in this community," and dispatched them to Choctaw communities "with instructions to explain to the identified full-bloods the benevolent nature of the government's offer." Smith was in Mississippi, he explained, for the purpose of "extending to the indigent ones, on behalf of the United States, such aid as may be necessary to assist them in getting their Indian rights."[17] The five agents were furnished with a team and driver each, were paid a wage of six dollars per day, and were obliged to transport the Choctaw to Meridian.

Smith realized that his task would be difficult. He was especially upset by the deceit of contractors from the Indian Territory, who were engaged in removing the full-bloods. Smith knew that the Choctaw were susceptible to the urgings of the speculators, since they had little money of their own and many of them were in debt to local merchants and farmers. "At least 99 percent of these Indians have not a dollar in the world," Smith reported to the Dawes commission. "There are now between sixty or seventy full-bloods here ready to remove to the Territory, and I do not find one of them able to go without assistance. Their household effects were brought to Meridian in one wagon."[18] This was a lucrative business, and it was certainly to the advantage of the speculators to dissuade the Choctaw from accepting the government's offer of transportation and rations. Smith reported to the commission on July 29 that contractors had already removed 1,100 Choctaw to the Indian Territory and "that they expect to have a thousand more between now and fall."[19] If this number was correct, then nearly all the Mississippi Choctaw would have been resettled in the Indian Territory and very few with the support of the government.

On August 12, Smith reported that some twenty-five to thirty Choctaw had been taken to Ardmore in the Chickasaw Nation by contractors in the spring and early summer and "were pretty roughly treated." They had returned to Mississippi and "reported to their neighbors that there is a great scarcity of water in the Choctaw and Chickasaw Nations and advised them not to go."[20] According to Julia K. Sparger, several hundred Choctaw from Mississippi had been taken to Ardmore in 1902. "Few preparations had been made for their care," she writes. "They were housed in unheated warehouses east of the Sante Fe tracks, and many died."[21] Since allotments would not be made until the Chickasaw and Choctaw Land Offices were opened on April 15, 1903, these Choctaw were required to wait nearly a year before they could be placed on their homesites.

Many of the Mississippi Choctaw were reluctant to leave because of debts owed to the farmers whose lands they sharecropped or to local merchants. Smith attempted to allay their fears. When the Reverend Jim Wallace of Eady wrote a letter on July 30 indicating that he desired to be removed to the Indian Territory but owed fifteen dollars to Floyd Cooper of Conehatta, Smith responded the next day that he could not pay the debt but would send Agent Gresset to explain the benefits that would accrue from removal. Smith noted in a letter to Gill Simpson of Edinburg on August 3 that she was "undecided on account of the condition of your crops" and encouraged her to emigrate west. Similar letters were sent on the same day to Wilson Isom of Edinburg, to James Ames and Martha Jasper of Melon, to Willie Solomon and John William of Baccus, to Jim Haney of Paulding, and to Hudson Lewis of Conehatta, all of whom were fearful that their crops would remain unharvested and that they would not be able to pay off their debts.[22]

In a letter to Joe Joshua of Saint Anns that was dated August 6, Smith referred to Joshua's earlier letter "stating that you are under contract to gather your crop, and that you have no way of paying him what you owe him until this crop is harvested." Joshua had asked whether the government would relieve him of his contract. Smith replied, "If you and your family go to the Indian Territory and secure allotments of land to which you are entitled, you will be better able to pay the debts to which you refer than by remaining in Mississippi." On August 6, Smith wrote to John William of Baccus, acknowledging William's complaint that he owed "about one hundred dollars which you will have to pay before you go to Indian Territory, and that so many men are after you wanting you to sign contracts, you would prefer to sell your claim in the Indian Territory and remain in Mississippi." Smith wrote that there was no provision in the law that would permit the government to pay William's debts. On August 4, Smith wrote to Rena Billey of Toles in order to persuade her to remove and to overcome her misgivings. "I understand that you wish to go to Choctaw-Chickasaw country," Smith said, "but are undecided on account of the condition of your crops." If Mrs. Billey and her three children wanted to preserve their rights, they must report to Smith in Meridian no later than Tuesday, August 11. "If you are unable to pay your own expenses," Smith added, "I will provide you and the members of your family with free transportation to the Territory and free rations as provided by law."[23]

There were other considerations. Sim Wickson of Eady wrote to Smith on August 1 to find out whether or not he could file for his wife in the Indian Territory, "because she did not want to emigrate." Smith responded that she would have to make settlement for herself. George Thomas of Sandersville inquired on August 6 whether he could receive lands in the West without actually going there, because his wife was too ill to travel. Smith replied, "There is no way by which you can secure these lands without your actual removal to the Indian Territory." When Smith discovered that George Simpson of Cushtusa had telephoned Green McCurtain, principal chief of the Oklahoma Choctaw, he wrote Simpson asking him to come to Meridian so that he could prove his authority as a federal agent.[24]

Smith hoped that he could remove the Indians inexpensively. He asked four railroad companies to bid on the contract for transporting the Mississippi Choctaw but was disappointed when all of the companies quoted the same flat rate of $11.50 for adults and $5.75 for children between the ages of five and twelve, with no charge for children under five. Each passenger would be allowed a maximum of 150 pounds of personal luggage; larger items would be shipped separately. When Smith discovered that the fare would not be lowered, he reluctantly accepted the bid of the Queen and Crescent Railway and ordered a special train to leave Meridian at 3:00 P.M., Wednesday, August 12.[25]

For five or six days before the departure date, the Choctaw began to arrive in Meridian. By August 10 Smith had confirmed the eligibility of about 150 Choctaw and was issuing rations at the county fairgrounds, three miles outside Meridian. "Being in absolute want," Smith reported later, "it was necessary to subsist them, which I did at a total cost of $179.90." A few of the arrivals became ill. Smith contracted with Dr. R. J. Sharman of Meridian to provide medical attention for a sum of $24 and purchased medicines from druggist Gus C. Kendall for $4.10.[26]

A number of speculators hovered about the campgrounds, offering "whiskey and money as inducements to sign contracts" and alleging that the government intended to place the Mississippi Choctaw on only the worst lands in the Choctaw and Chickasaw nations. On August 10, Smith issued a special notice, warning the Choctaw not to sign contracts with speculators and advising them that the government would "protect them from unscrupulous persons whose aim is to take advantage of the Indian."[27] Smith reported that he was worried about the effect of speculators upon the Choctaw gathered at the fairgrounds. "I am informed by very reliable parties," he wrote,

> that many merchants and farmers with whom these Indians have been trading for years, and on whom they have been in a nature dependent, are bitterly opposed to the removal of the Indians from Mississippi. It is alleged that they have done all in their power to keep the Indians from moving, and in one letter received it was reported that a number of Choctaws had been told I had no authority from the Government to remove them to the Indian Territory, and that it was merely an excuse to entice them to Meridian and have them sign contracts for the sale of their prospective allotments in the Indian Territory. The time being so short and the means of communication so uncertain, it was impossible for me to notify all Choctaws whose time for removal to the Indian Territory expires August 14th, that these and similar reports were absolutely false and circulated only for the purpose of misleading and confusing the Indians.[28]

Late on the evening of August 11, handbills were circulated around Meridian, announcing that a stickball game would be held at ten

The Second Choctaw Removal, 1903

o'clock the next morning. Smith had previously notified the Choctaw that they were to have their baggage packed and ready to be moved to the depot in Meridian early that morning. "This ball game greatly interfered with those plans," Smith informed the Dawes commission. He investigated the matter and found that a speculator named Edwards from Ardmore had arranged the game in hopes of causing excitement and dissension among the Choctaw, thereby delaying their removal and inducing them "to desert their friends and go to the Indian Territory with him." Smith went to the fairgrounds early in the morning and "explained the matter to the leading Indians, the result being that the ball game was declared off, and I succeeded in getting all the Indians and baggage to the depot and started on the trip to the Territory by five o'clock this afternoon."[29]

On the afternoon of August 12, a special train of the Queen and Crescent Railway left Meridian with 259 full-blood Choctaw. Five more Indians would be picked up that evening in Monroe, Louisiana. Of these emigrants, 169 were over the age of twelve, 48 were between five and twelve, and 47 were under the age of five. A few infants born after April 30, 1903, were not listed by the Dawes commission. The oldest of the passengers was Solomon Jackson, age eighty-two, from Stamper in Newton County. Fifty-eight emigrants came from Tucker. Toles in Kemper County provided thirty-two; Engine, thirty-nine; Cushtusa in Neshoba County, twenty; Conehatta in Newton County, forty-two; and Union in Newton County, thirteen. All of these communities had been much involved in missionary and educational programs, suggesting that those Choctaw who left for the Indian Territory were among the more highly educated.[30]

The Dawes commission had selected Atoka in the western part of the Choctaw Nation as a campsite for the Mississippi Choctaw until they could be settled on their homesteads. It was conveniently located on the line of the Missouri, Kansas, and Texas Railway, and the Choctaw Land Office had been established there. William H. Angell, the commissioner of the Land Office, reported to the Dawes commission on August 8 that, in his judgment, "conditions as to water and other facilities are favorable here for encampment of four hundred Indians."[31] On August 13, Angell wrote the commission that arrangements had been made for a camp at Smallwood's Switch, three miles south of Atoka. "I have personally examined this location," he re-

Stickball as it is played each year by teams at the Choctaw Fair and at informal gatherings. *Photo: Mary Ann Wells*

ported, "and find that there are ample camping facilities and an abundant supply of water." Angell expected to proceed with allotments for the newcomers "as soon as it is practicable and to ascertain such land in this locality as has not heretofore been selected by, or is now being held in the lawful possession of any other citizen, freedmen or identified Mississippi Choctaw." He also reported that the section of land bounded on the north by the Arkansas and Choctaw Railroad, on the south by the Red River, on the west by the Missouri, Kansas, and Texas Railway, and on the east by the St. Louis and San Francisco Railroad, was "a strip of country well adapted for agricultural purposes," despite the fact that much of it was heavily wooded and had been used primarily for livestock. He intended to make arbitrary allotments to the Choctaw who were arriving from Mississippi, since he did not believe it necessary for them to "see the land, and it is probable that a selection more to their interest and benefit can be made by our special agents without incurring the expense of carrying these Indians to see the land until after allotment has arbitrarily been made." To meet this goal Angell sent Carl Patterson to prepare plats and report on the condition of the land.[32] On August 13 Angell informed Patterson that it was the desire of the commission "to secure the expeditious settlement and allotment of these Indians at the earliest practicable date as the United States Government is under moral obligation to provide for the sustenance of these Indians until such time as they are able to provide for themselves."[33]

Precisely at midnight, August 13, the special train from Meridian arrived at Atoka.[34] The passengers were required to stay overnight on the train, and the next morning they were taken to the campsite at Smallwood's Switch. The Dawes commission had erected nine-by-nine-foot tents as shelter, had contracted with the Atoka firm of Reynolds and Sample to provide rations, and provided utensils for the Choctaw to use in preparing food.[35]

On August 17, Angell reported that the camp was in good condition and that "there had been but little sickness among the Indians that might be attributed to camp life." He added ominously, however, "There have been two deaths, both of which, however, were the results of diseases contracted in Mississippi."[36] On September 9, Angell informed Special Agent Smith that he had contracted the services of

Doctors J. S. Fulton and T. J. Long of Atoka. "A large number of these Indians," especially children, he reported, "have been sick with chills and fever, diarrhea, flux, colds, and in some instances threatened with pneumonia. . . ." By this time four of the children had died, and Angell feared that an epidemic might break out among the emigrants. "I did not deem it wise to take any chances," Angell declared, "which might in any way be attributed to lack of medical attention, and thus subject the Commission to criticism."[37]

On September 2, the Choctaw Land office finally made allotments to sixty-six of the Mississippi Choctaw, but these had to be approved by the Dawes commission in Muskogee. Angell reported to the commission on September 5 that a temporary camp was to be established at Bennington in Blue County and that he could take those who had been assigned allotments to that point by wagon as soon as tents and tools had been provided for each family. By September 14, the commission had approved the allotments. This first group of Mississippi Choctaw was escorted by William W. Folsom of Atoka to Bennington on the following day. The Bennington Mercantile Company was awarded a contract to provide rations, and Thomas Bayless was given the job of placing the Choctaw on their homesteads.[38]

On September 14, Angell instructed Bayless to locate the newcomers on their allotments by families. When Bayless later complained that he was having difficulty doing so, Angell admonished him to "simply take the Mississippi Choctaws who are down with you there, and place them on their allotments, and if they are alarmed over the situation and are unable to secure water conveniently you can allow them to come back and stay in the camp." Angell insisted, "You should impress upon them the advisability of remaining on their allotments if possible and building a cabin." To aid the Choctaw in building these houses and to clear their land, the commission purchased tools for each family: one hammer, one axe, one saw, one hatchet, and one frow, at a cost of three dollars for each set.[39]

On September 29, Angell wrote to Special Agent Smith, asking him to purchase additional tents for the Choctaw at Bennington until their cabins were constructed. "I am afraid," he declared, "that they are not much at home building, and that they will be left without shelter entirely." On the same day, Angell wrote to Bayless urging him to place the Mississippi Choctaw on their allotments as quickly as possible and to "advise them that it will be necessary to build a house within a week or ten days in order that you may secure the tent to loan to other Indians." Angell was anticipating the arrival of another trainload of Choctaw from Mississippi, who were scheduled to arrive in early October.[40]

Bayless continued to report difficulties. He informed the Land Office that some of the homesteads did not have an adequate water supply and that, without either wagons or barrels, the Choctaw could not haul water to their homesites and were forced back to the camp at Bennington. The newcomers also encountered another problem, one with explosive potential. According to Bayless, some of the local Oklahoma Choctaw and intermarried whites threatened the Mississippi Choctaw "when they are placed on the land and the Government officials have left Bennington," causing many of them to abandon their allotments.[41]

At this time the Land Office had come to recognize that the Bennington area did not have sufficient land for allotments to all of the Mississippi Choctaw. Angell recommended that land in the vicinity of Boswell and Soper be assigned and that another camp be established at the Honey Springs Church just south of Soper. On October 6 the Dawes commission approved this proposal and ordered that 136 of the Mississippi Choctaw still at Atoka be transported to the new location. Forty would be taken to Bennington, where they would join the 83 who had already been placed on their allotments. On October 7, Agent Smith escorted an additional 26 Choctaw from Meridian to the Indian Territory. This group was taken to Fort Towson, on the line of the St. Louis and San Francisco Railroad, and would be taken later to the camp near Soper. The government then abandoned its efforts to bring additional Mississippi Choctaw to the Indian Territory, as the time period authorized by the supplementary agreement of 1902 had expired. On October 21, the camp at Atoka was disbanded after its occupants were finally transferred to either Bennington or Soper. Not until the spring of 1904, however, were all of the Choctaw who had emigrated with the support of the federal government placed on their allotments.[42]

The 290 Choctaw were but a small portion of all the Mississippi and Louisiana Choctaw who were removed to the Indian Territory prior to the closing of the tribal rolls in 1907. By this date the Dawes commission had confirmed the settlement in Oklahoma of 1,462 Mississippi Choctaw. After the rolls were reopened to admit newborns and to include persons who successfully contested their citizenship, another 177 Mississippi Choctaw were added to the list of emigrants.[43] Although a considerable number of these Choctaw would return to Mississippi, it is clear that the number of Choctaw in that state had drastically declined.

The diminution of numbers was accompanied by major changes in the direction of Mississippi Choctaw society. Whole communities had chosen to leave for the Indian Territory, and many of the ministers who had served them had also chosen to relocate. Many of the Baptist and Methodist churches, and the schools that they sponsored, were abandoned or were greatly reduced in numbers. Of the Methodist churches, for example, only Simson Tubby's mission at Black Jack remained intact. Nearly all of the Choctaw who had been attached to the Catholic mission at Tucker departed for the West and, according to one report, all of the mission staff except one left with them. This mission gradually recovered as other Choctaw were persuaded to till its agricultural lands, but it was never restored to the condition in which it had been before 1903. The state of Mississippi, responding to the decline in Choctaw population, also abandoned its efforts to provide schooling for the Choctaw. The communities were therefore badly shaken when the more educated Choctaw departed for the Indian Territory. Those who remained in Mississippi fell into another period of isolation. Only after 1918 and the establishment of a federal agency for the Choctaw would the Indians regain the direction and momentum that they had had in the two decades before the second removal.

Notes

1. A complete list of all 264 Mississippi and Louisiana Choctaw who emigrated to the Choctaw Nation on August 12–13, 1903, may be found at the Federal Archives and Records Center (FARC), Fort Worth, Texas, in Record Group 75, Bureau of Indian Affairs, Records of the Commission to the Five Civilized Tribes (CFCT), Records Relating to Mississippi Choctaw, Entry 112, Lists of Persons Removed.

2. Statistics regarding the removal of Mississippi Choctaw appear in the *Annual Report* of the commissioner of Indian affairs (hereafter cited as ARCIA) for the year 1907, pp. 11–12; the story of the removal and the settlement in Indian Territory may be traced

in ARCIA for the years 1903, 1904, 1905, and 1906 as well, and in John H. Peterson, Jr., "The Mississippi Band of Choctaw Indians: Their Recent History and Current Social Relations" (Ph.D. diss., University of Georgia, 1970), 90–108. A summary of enrollment also appears in Joseph W. Howell, Report Relating to the Enrollment of Citizens and Freedmen of the Five Civilized Tribes, to the Secretary of the Interior, March 3, 1909, Choctaw Removal Records, Record Group 75, National Archives.

3. A convenient summary of treaty rights and other pertinent legislation regarding the Mississippi Choctaw appears in John William Wade, "The Removal of the Mississippi Choctaws," *Publications of the Mississippi Historical Society* 8 (1904): 404–6; also see Angie Debo, *The Rise and Fall of the Choctaw Republic* (Norman: University of Oklahoma Press, 1934), 273–76; Peterson, "The Mississippi Band of Choctaw Indians," 93–94; and ARCIA for 1899, pp,. 73–77, and 1898, 423–33.

4. Background on the condition of Mississippi Choctaw in the two decades prior to the removal of 1903 is given in Edward Davis, "The Mississippi Choctaws," *Chronicles of Oklahoma* 10 (June 1932): 257–66; Charlie Mitchell Beckett, "Choctaw Indians in Mississippi since 1830" (master's thesis, Oklahoma Agricultural and Mechanical College, 1949); Bobby Thomspon and John H. Peterson, Jr., "Mississippi Choctaw Identity: Genesis and Change," in *The New Ethnicity*, ed. John W. Bennett (St. Paul: West, 1975), 179–96; and especially in Peterson, "The Mississippi Band of Choctaw Indians."

5. The best accounts of Baptist and Methodist mission work among the Choctaw appear in the dissertation by Peterson and the thesis by Beckett, but also see A. B. Brown, *History of Newton County, Mississippi, from 1834 to 1894* (Jackson: Clarion-Ledger, 1894), 10–11; and Eugene I. Farr, "A History of Baptist Missions among the Choctaw Indians of the Bogue Homa Reservation" (master's thesis, Baptist Bible Institute, New Orleans, Louisiana, 1942).

6. Reverend Richard Oliver Gerow, *Catholicity in Mississippi* (Natchez: Hope Haven Press, 1939), 260–63. The most complete account of the mission at Tucker is in Peterson, "The Mississippi Band of Choctaw Indians," 77–78.

7. The development of state schools for the Mississippi Choctaw can be followed in the reports of H. S. Halbert, "Indian Schools in Mississippi," in *Biennial Report of the State Superintendent of Public Education to the Legislature of Mississippi for Scholastic Years 1891–92 and 1892–93* (Jackson: Clarion-Ledger, 1894), 574–76; Halbert, "The Indians in Mississippi and Their Schools," in *Biennial Report of the State Superintendent of Public Education to the Legislature of Mississippi for Scholastic Years 1893–94 and 1894–95* (Jackson: Clarion-Ledger, 1895), 534–41; Halbert, "Indian Schools," in *Biennial Report of the State Superintendent of Public Education to the Legislature of Mississippi for Scholastic Years 1895–96 and 1896–97* (Jackson: Clairion-Ledger, 1898), 23–30; and Halbert, "The Mississippi Choctaws," in *Biennial Report of the State Superintendent of Public Education to the Legislature of Mississippi for Scholastic Years 1897–98 and 1898–99* (Jacksonville, Fla.: Vance, 1900), 35–38.

8. These initial efforts at removal in the early 1890s and the role of Standley are discussed in Peterson, "The Mississippi Band of Choctaw Indians," 91; Davis, "The Mississippi Choctaws," 261–62; Debo, *The Rise and Fall of the Choctaw Republic*, 181. Pertinent documents may be found in U.S. Congress, *Mississippi Choctaws*, 54th Cong., 2d sess., March 3, 1897, H. Rpt. 3080.

9. Davis, "The Mississippi Choctaws," 264; Jesse O. McKee and Jon A. Schlenker, *The Choctaws: Cultural Evolution of a Native American Tribe* (Jackson: University Press of Mississippi, 1980), 93, 97–98; and ARCIA for 1898, 1899, and 1900.

10. Howell, Report Relating to the Enrollment, 188; ARCIA for 1902 and 1903.

11. Peterson, "The Mississippi Band of Choctaw Indians," 94; Beckett, "Choctaw Indians in Mississippi since 1830," 46; ARCIA for 1906, p. 32.

12. Davis, "The Mississippi Choctaws," 264; ARCIA for 1899, pp. 77–80; 1902, pp. 523–24; adn 1905, pp. 22–23.

13. *ARCIA* for 1903, p. 93; and 1904, p. 19.
14. E. A. Hitchcock, Secretary of the Interior, to the CFCT, July 2, 1903, Records of the Dawes Commission, Oklahoma Historical Society, reel 61.
15. Thomas B. Needles, Commissioner in Charge, to the Honorable Tams Bixby, July 22, 1903, and July 24, 1903, in Records of the Dawes Commission.
16. H. Van V. Smith to CFCT, July 29, 1903, in Letters Sent by Special Agent Smith, Ledger 1, July 1903, in RG 75, FARC, Fort Worth, Entry 168.
17. Ibid.
18. Ibid.
19. Ibid.
20. Ibid., August 12, 1903.
21. Julia K. Sparger, "Young Ardmore," *Chronicles of Oklahoma* 43, no. 4 (Winter 1965–66):409–10.
22. Smith to the Reverend Jim Wallace, Smith to Gill Simpson, Smith to Wilson Isom, Smith to James Ames, Smith to Martha Jasper, Smith to Willie Solomon, Smith to John William, Smith to Jim Haney, and Smith to Hudson Lewis, all dated August 3, 1903, Letters Sent by Special Agent Smith, Ledgers 1 and 2, RG 75, FARC, Forth Worth, Entry 168.
23. Smith to Joe Joshua, August 6, 1903, Smith to John William, August 6, 1903, and Smith to Rena Billey, August 4, 1903, in ibid.
24. Smith to Sim Wickson, August 4, 1903, Smith to George Thomas, August 6, 1903, Smith to George Simpson, August 6, 1903, in ibid.
25. Smith, telegrams to C. M. Shepard, General Purchasing Agent, Mobile and Ohio Railroad; to George H. Smith, General Purchasing Agent, Queen and Crescent Railway; to James Hagerman, General Solicitor, Missouri, Kansas, and Texas Railroad; and to L. F. Parker, General Solicitor, St. Louis and San Francisco Railroad, all on August 6, 1903; Smith to George H. Smith, August 12, 1903, and Smith to CFCT, August 12, 1903, all in ibid.
26. Smith to CFCT, August 10, 12, and September 19, 1903, and Smith to Rees Evans, August 24, 1903, in ibid.
27. Smith to CFCT, August 10, 1903, in ibid.
28. Smith to CFCT, August 12, 1903, in ibid.
29. Ibid.
30. Ibid. The total cost of transportation is specified in Smith to CFCT, September 19, 1903. The gender, ages, and addresses of the emigrants may be found in Entry 112, Lists of Persons Removed.
31. William H. Angell, Commissioner of the Choctaw Land Office, to CFCT, August 8, 1903, in Records of the Choctaw Land Office, RG 75, FARC, Fort Worth, Entry 165.
32. Ibid., Angell to CFCT, August 13, 1903.
33. Ibid., Angell to Carl Patterson, August 13, 1903.
34. Smith to Rees Evans, telegrams, August 13, 1903; to CFCT, August 14, 1903; to the Commissioner of Indian Affairs, August 16, 1903; and letter to CFCT, August 15, 1903, Letters Sent by Special Agent Smith, Ledger 2, RG 75, FARC, Fort Worth, Entry 168.
35. Ibid., Smith to Rees Evans, August 24, 1903, Smith to Reynolds and Sample, telegram, August 18, 1903; "A Big Contract," *Indian Citizen*, August 20, 1903.
36. Angell to CFCT, August 17, 1903, Records of the Choctaw Land Office, RG 75, FARC, Fort Worth, Entry 165.
37. Ibid., Angell to CFCT, September 9, 1903.
38. Ibid., Angell to CFCT, September 5, 14, 29, 1903.
39. Ibid., Angell to Thomas Bayless, September 14, 1903.
39. Ibid., Angell to Thomas Bayless, September 14, 1903.

40. Ibid., Angell to Smith, September 29, 1903, and Angell to Bayless, September 29, 1903.
41. Ibid., Bayless to Choctaw Land Office, September 22, 29, 1903.
42. Ibid., Angell to Smith, September 30, October 3, 1903; "More Mississippi Choctaws," *Indian Citizen*, October 15, 1903.
43. Commissioner of Indian Affairs, *Report*, 1907 60th Cong., 1st sess., H. Doc. 5.; Howell, Report Relating to the Enrollment.

7

Holy Rosary Indian Mission: The Mississippi Choctaw and the Catholic Church

Sister John Christopher Langford, M.S.B.T.

The Mississippi Choctaw were a scattered remnant of a once proud nation living as outcasts in their ancestral homeland when the Catholic church established its first missions in Neshoba County in 1843. Not until 1881, however, when the newly appointed bishop of Natchez, Right Reverend Francis Janssens, made an inspection tour of his immense diocese, which included the entire state of Mississippi, did the true plight of the Choctaw become apparent to the churchman.[1]

Janssens discovered that most Choctaw earned their livelihoods through sharecropping, day labor, or subsistence farming. A few were employed in the lumber industry. Disease and malnutrition shortened their life expectancy; educational opportunities were largely nonexistent; and the U.S. government did not recognize the Mississippi Choctaw as a tribe. The bishop was so deeply moved that he soon afterward made a trip to Holland in search of a missionary to minister to the special needs of the Mississippi Choctaw.[2]

Father B. J. Bekkers, pastor of a thriving parish in Amsterdam, answered Bishop Janssens's plea. Father Bekkers arrived in Neshoba County in November 1883 and took up residence with the J. Holland family.[3] The Dutch priest's first task was to establish himself as part of the Indian community and to overcome the Choctaw suspicion of white men. He contacted Tom Billy, the Choctaw community miko, or chief, and tried to explain his purposes in coming to Mississippi. At first Chief Tom Billy said that he was not interested in the priest's plans, but on the Sunday following their first talk, his son, Willy, attended mass when it was celebrated in the Holland residence.

Gradually a bond of respect and trust grew between the two men as Father Bekkers told Chief Billy of his plans to build a church and a school as well as to provide material assistance whenever possible. The church's plan to purchase 2,037 acres of land in Neshoba County and parcel it out to Choctaw families in forty-acre units further strengthened the growing ties. After the miko had agreed to move his family onto church land, other individuals—among them Willie Phillips, Jim Jack, Old Jefferson, and Bernard Simpson—followed.[4] They all agreed to give a fifth of their produce to help defray church expenses in return for use of the land. These men and their families formed the nucleus of the Indian community at Tucker.

Less than a year later, on July 30, 1884, the community started building a church. Moving quickly to finish the work before it was time to harvest the crops, the men managed to dedicate the building and consecrate the bell on September 10. The church was given the name Holy Rosary in honor of Our Lady of the Rosary.

Father Bekkers and his Choctaw congregation invited Bishop Janssens for the dedication, which was a joyous occasion, with games of stickball and chunky after mass. Chief Billy, Father Bekkers, and the other individuals who had contributed to the building of the church and the growth of the community expressed their happiness with the mission's progress and their optimism about the future. An enormous feast completed the celebration.

Progress was being made on the educational front as well. Seven days after the church building had been dedicated, Henry Halbert opened the Catholic school at Tucker and became its first teacher. Since English was not the children's native language, Halbert immediately set about learning Choctaw to enhance not only his teaching skills but also his ability to communicate. Attendance was low when the school first opened, because it was harvest time and the children were needed to help pick cotton, but the student body grew as soon as the crop had been hauled to the gin.

In the meantime Father Bekkers had come to rely more and more on the strength and guidance of Chief Billy, who was now widely regarded as a friend to the priest and as an important, influential example within

SISTER JOHN CHRISTOPHER LANGFORD, M.S.B.T.

Holy Rosary Mission in 1933. *Photo: Bureau of Indian Affairs*

the community. He was the interpreter ally. Chief Billy also explained the customs, ceremonies, and traditions of his people to Father Bekkers and to other individuals. He aided the pastor by apportioning civic duties as well as settling conflicts among the congregation. Billy's reputation for integrity and fairness made his decisions readily acceptable to everyone. Community leaders after him became known as "church mikos," holding a position attained by moral example within the community. The church mikos were interpreters and catechists who explained the doctrine of the church to their people and told them how to relate it to their lives. By their example they inspired others to good works. They aided the pastor by apportioning civic duties as well as by settling conflicts among the congregation.

Father Bekkers and the Sisters of Mercy, who had come to teach in the school, made the Choctaw welcome in both the rectory and the convent. When there was sickness or trouble, the little religious community met and prayed. Soon the church and school had become the community center, a place where the Tucker Choctaw gathered to socialize and to discuss common problems. On Saturday afternoon families arrived by wagon at the church, went to the sacrament of confession, and camped in the woods overnight. The following morning they attended high mass. Men segregated themselves on one side of the church, wearing high paper collars on their shirts and squirrel tails attached to their belts. Women wore long calico dresses and brightly colored kerchiefs and sat together, across the aisle from the men.[5] After the mass they conversed, played ball, and ate picnic lunches, which were called "dinner-on-the-ground" throughout the area. On Sunday afternoon they returned to the church for "Benediction of the Blessed Sacrament", and afterward hitched up their teams to travel home.[6]

Slowly the mission grew. Choctaw from nearby communities came for instruction and were baptized. Toward the latter part of the century, Father Bekkers began searching for someone to take over his duties at the mission. He believed there was enough work for a community of priests and brothers. During the spring of 1898 he visited Europe and enlisted the aid of the Carmelite priests and brothers. When they joined Father Bekkers in Mississippi, he helped initiate them into their new work.[7] The Sisters of Mercy continued their regular assignments at Holy Rosary, and the church assigned Father Bekkers to the pastorate in Meridian.

The turn of the century brought a number of events that seemed to conspire against the well-being of the Mississippi Choctaw and the growth of Holy Rosary Mission. In August 1900, Chief Billy died just as the U.S. government began to renew its efforts to settle all Choctaw in Indian Territory, present-day Oklahoma. The federal government cut off all appropriations to Catholic Indian schools, including food and aid for education.[8] At the same time the government offered the Mississippi Choctaw the opportunity to claim 160 acres of land per family, plus farm equipment and seed, if they took up residence in Indian Territory.[9] Many Choctaw preferred to remain in Mississippi, but even with the intervention of people such as Father William H. Ketcham, the director of the Catholic Indian Missions in Washington, D.C., the Indians were helpless to resist the pressures of the federal government. Most of the Choctaw left Tucker, accompanied by the Carmelite priests. The school closed, and the Sisters of Mercy returned to Vicksburg.

SISTER JOHN CHRISTOPHER LANGFORD, M.S.B.T.

Despite the efforts of the government to remove the Choctaw to Indian Territory, a small persistent group numbering not many more than a thousand refused to leave their ancestral lands in Mississippi. The church continued to minister to these people, with Father Enis as pastor of Holy Rosary from 1904 to 1913. In time the Catholic school was reopened and a lay teacher was put in charge.

Some of the Mississippi Choctaw who migrated to Indian Territory discovered the land there to be meager and unproductive. Many of them returned home to Neshoba County, settling on mission land, which was still the property of the diocese of Natchez. Many had been weakened by tuberculosis, had lost all they owned, and had been denied any further government aid when they left the reservation in Indian Territory. There was little work for them in Mississippi except as agricultural day laborers or sharecroppers.

Father Ketcham continued to prove himself a friend of the Choctaw. If his attempts at political intervention failed, his efforts to strengthen the Choctaw voice within the church succeeded. He translated a catechism of the Catholic religion into the Choctaw language to improve religious instruction, and *KIAHLIK IKSA NANA-AIYIMMIKA I KATIKISMA* was published in 1916.[10] The book contains basic Catholic prayers, information about sacraments, doctrine, and morality, and five Choctaw hymns. The information is presented in both English and Choctaw.

In about 1913 Monsignor Ketcham received a government appointment to the Board of Indian Commissioners, which served as a consultative body to the Bureau of Indian Affairs. In October 1917 he and other members of the commission made an official inspection of all the Choctaw settlements in Mississippi. Their recommendations resulted in the Indian Act, passed on May 25, 1918. For the first time since the Treaty of Dancing Rabbit Creek, the Mississippi Choctaw were an officially recognized tribe.

The Indian Act provided for a special physician-agent, a farmer, and a field nurse to come to Neshoba County to assist the Mississippi Choctaw. The act further provided funds to establish a day school, to acquire farmland, and to purchase as much as $75,000 in seed, animals, tools, and farm equipment. The government also promised that similar amounts would be forthcoming in succeeding years. The Mississippi

Holy Rosary Indian Mission

Choctaw Agency was also established in 1918, with Dr. John McKinley as the superintendent.[11] That same year the Catholic school at Tucker burned down, and Dr. McKinley began negotiating for the purchase of mission land so that a government day school could be built.

Meanwhile, Ketcham continued his efforts on behalf of the Mississippi Choctaw. He and Bishop Gunn, who now administered the Natchez diocese, perceived a need to formulate a long-term plan that would consolidate the recent advances of the Mississippi Choctaw and would provide a basis for further growth. Their first priority was to locate a religious community which would assume the duties at Holy Rosary. They were fortunate in attracting the Congregation of the Immaculate Heart of Mary, often called the Scheut Fathers and Brothers. This community had the resources to support its own parishes and missions. Furthermore, the members' experience in agriculture, Ketcham and Gunn thought, would help the Choctaw. In April 1921, Father Edmond Philippe and Brother Joseph Verhoven of the Congregation of the Immaculate Heart of Mary arrived in Tucker.

During the winter of 1921, Ketcham made an official inspection tour of all the Indian communities in Mississippi. The monsignor was not well but, feeling an urgent need to complete plans for the mission, continued in his duties. He and Father Philippe drew up plans for the future of the Indian mission. They agreed that the larger group of Choctaw at Stratton, Standing Pine, and Pearl River should be visited on a regular basis. It seemed unwise to build chapels in the outlying areas, however, because of the strong anti-Catholic feeling among whites nearby at that time.[12] Rather than risk the destruction of a chapel, they decided instead to purchase an automobile and to search for a Choctaw catechist to serve these areas by teaching Catholic fundamentals. Such a helper would already understand the language and customs of the Choctaw.

On Sunday morning, November 13, 1921, Monsignor Ketcham celebrated mass at Holy Rosary. The next day he collapsed and died. The Choctaw mourned the loss of Wamoli Wakita (Watchful Eagle), as they had affectionately called him.[13] The priests' plans for the mission continued to advance, however, as three sisters from the Community of the Canonesses Missionaries of Saint Augustine offered their services to the mission. Their offer was warmly received, and soon the sisters began teaching, nursing, and visiting in Choctaw homes. They also worked in the mission's dispensary until a government Indian hospital opened in Philadelphia in 1928. By that time many more Choctaw families had moved to Tucker and had been given at least twenty acres per family to farm. The plans to start large-scale farming of cotton and corn on mission land, however, had to be abandoned because of the expense and the lack of available land. In 1923 Father Philippe started a program to build an auditorium as a social center for young people. Movies were shown, and cooking and dressmaking classes were also held in the facility. The sisters taught the classes in addition to their other duties.

In 1928 the Bureau of Indian Affairs made a concerted effort to bring together the scattered Choctaw families and to settle them in larger communities where economic, educational, and medical assistance could be more easily administered. Pearl River, Standing Pine, Redwater, and Conehatta were given precedence over Tucker, which ceased to grow.

On September 4, 1930, the Canonesses Missionaries of St. Augustine left Tucker. They were followed in November by Father Philippe, who expressed the hope that goodwill and friendship would be maintained between Catholics and other Christians in the area. He also hoped that the Catholic church would keep the mission land to benefit the Choctaw. Father Philippe was replaced by Father J. T. McKenna, a diocesan priest.[14] After his first year at Tucker, Father McKenna found it necessary to bring another community of sisters to Holy Rosary. He called upon the newly formed Missionary Servants of the Most Blessed Trinity, and this community, founded in the U.S., answered the plea by sending three sisters in 1931. The sisters quickly became involved in teaching, home visiting, and home nursing as ways to nurture the Catholic faith among the Choctaw.

By 1934 the sisters were also teaching in the white public school during the regular class hours. They spent the after-school hours and weekends doing social work and offering religious education to the Choctaw. They taught sewing, knitting, and housekeeping skills.[15] Father McKenna remained a pastor of Holy Rosary Mission until 1937, when he, in turn, was replaced by Father Francis Deignan, who served there until 1944.[16]

Holy Rosary Indian Mission

In the same year, the Missionary Servants of the Most Holy Trinity took charge of the mission. This religious family of priests, brothers, and sisters has continued to serve at Holy Rosary until the present time. One member of this community, Brother Theodore Jurdt, has worked with the Choctaw for the entire period.

During the 1940s and 1950s, the Catholic church continued to cling to its long traditions. Rosary devotions, novenas, stations of the cross, and benedictions were attended regularly. The local parish provided socials, dances, bingo, baseball, scouting, dinners, and other activities which brought families together.

During this time, Father Donald Lynch wrote about the mission for church publications, describing the duties of the church miko, who was then Willie Solomon.[17] Lynch also wrote about problems confronting the parish.[18] The large area required a sixty-mile round trip to serve the missions in Tucker, Pearl River, and Conehatta. He noted that the government's educational programs for Indian youth did not equip them with the skills necessary to improve the tribe's economy. On the positive side, Lynch observed that a love of family life united many Choctaw. He was particularly impressed with the Choctaw's deep respect for their dead, their belief in the power of prayer, and their high regard for action rather than words.

Then, in the 1960s, the Catholic church went through a period of renewal and reform. The church reevaluated its traditions and made changes in symbols and signs. At first these changes caused some confusion and discomfort, but they eventually enabled the laity to participate more fully in the ceremonies. The changes at Holy Rosary Mission were varied. The church was remodeled and the altar placed in a prominent position. English replaced Latin as the church language, and many rituals were revised to allow greater participation. Choctaw culture was integrated with these changes whenever possible, and parish councils were formed to discuss education, worship, finance, and social concerns. The office of church chief was retained and strengthened, and the holder of the office became a representative at various parish and diocesan meetings and functions. Choctaw hymns were sung in mass, and native symbols were used on banners and in altar coverings.

Since the arrival of the Missionary Servant of the Most Blessed

SISTER JOHN CHRISTOPHER LANGFORD, M.S.B.T.

Holy Rosary Mission in 1984. *Photo: William Brescia*

Trinity in 1931, more than sixty sisters have served at Holy Rosary. For more than fifteen years Sister Rose Anita worked and served as religious and public school teacher, also providing food and clothing to those in need of emergency relief. There are now three sisters at Holy Rosary. One of them, Sister Joan Lorraine Kreutz, is employed by the Bureau of Indian Affairs as a classroom teacher at Tucker Day School. The other two sisters are engaged in religious education and pastoral ministry. Sister Virginia Ann Wagner was employed by the Indian Health Service from 1978 to 1984 and served as director of the outpatient clinic at the Choctaw Health Center for two years.

Father Thaddeus Searles was pastor at Holy Rosary parish during the implementation of post–Vatican II renewal. He encouraged greater self-determination for the Choctaw, provided additional educational opportunities, and collaborated with tribal leaders. Father Robert Goodyear joined the mission in 1975. He works closely with the human services agencies in support of social justice in all areas of Choctaw life. Goodyear learned the Choctaw language and, on May 1, 1983, cele-

Holy Rosary Indian Mission

brated the first Choctaw mass in the Conehatta community. Since then he has celebrated mass in Choctaw at Tucker and Conehatta.

Holy Rosary Mission has served the Mississippi Choctaw for more than a century. The relationship between the church and the Choctaw has been close and mutually supportive, strengthened by memories of past sorrows and joys and encouraged by hopes for the future. Throughout this long relationship the mission has assisted the Choctaw in their struggle to remain a separate and proud people. The church has continuously respected the dignity of the Choctaw people while also understanding the need for economic assistance. This support has been provided through the early land acquisition programs, the extensive educational efforts, and the furtherance of community practices in mission buildings. Whatever the future holds, the Choctaw people and the church will share it together.

Notes

1. Victor C. Declercq, *The Scheut Fathers in the U.S.A.* (Arlington, Va.: Missionhurst, 1978), 27.
2. Mother Mary Bernard, *The Story of the Sisters of Mercy in Mississippi* (New York: Kennedy and Sons, 1931), 124.
3. Declercq, *Scheut Fathers*, 27.
4. Bernard, *Sisters of Mercy*, 127.
5. Ibid., 128.
6. Reverend Franz-Bernard Lickteig, O. Carm., "The Choctaw Indian Apostolate," *Sword* 19, no. 2 (June 1969):69.
7. Bernard, *Sisters of Mercy*, 137.
8. Lickteig, "The Choctaw Indian Apostolate," 42.
9. Ibid.
10. William H. Ketcham, *Kiahlik Iksa Nana-Aiyimmika I Katikisma* (Washington, D.C.: Bureau of Catholic Missions, 1916).
11. Declerq, *Scheut Fathers*, 29.
12. Ibid., 54.
13. Ibid., 52.
14. Reverend Richard O. Gerow, *Catholicity in Mississippi* (Marrero, Louisiana: Hope Haven Press, 1939), 26.
15. George Moreland, "Life on the Indian Reservation," *Memphis Commercial Appeal*, April 29, 1934.
16. Gerow, *Catholicity in Mississippi*, 262.
17. Reverend Donald Lynch, "The Choctaws," *Missionary Servant Magazine*, September 1950, p. 12.
18. Reverend Donald Lynch, "Hali-to Means Hello," *Missionary Servant Magazine*, December 1952, p. 20.

8

Economic Progress and Development of the Choctaw since 1945

Jesse O. McKee and Steve Murray

The Mississippi Choctaw's most important success in modern times has been progress in the economic development of their reservation. The main influences leading to this development have been increased educational opportunities for all Choctaw and the federal government's policy of self-determination, which has given American Indians an increasing voice in their own destiny.

The federal government has at different times appeared to be the Choctaw's best friend and worse enemy in the long battle for self-sufficiency in the twentieth century. After its discovery of extreme poverty among the Choctaw in the early part of the century, the U.S. government appeared to be acting with compassion when the Bureau of Indian Affairs (BIA) established the Choctaw Indian Agency at Philadelphia in 1918. The government authorized $75,000 to assist the Choctaw in economic development, education, and health. These funds were to go directly toward the purchase of supplies, farmland, and education.

In 1920 a day school program was started, and by 1930 elementary schools had been established in all seven communities. Progress in health services began in 1926 with the establishment of a thirty-five-bed Indian hospital in Philadelphia. A land purchase program began in 1921 and eventually led to the establishment of a reservation for the

We wish to thank Roger Anderson, Albert Farve, Bob Ferguson, and especially Robert Benn for their time and assistance in providing us with some of the information needed to write this chapter.

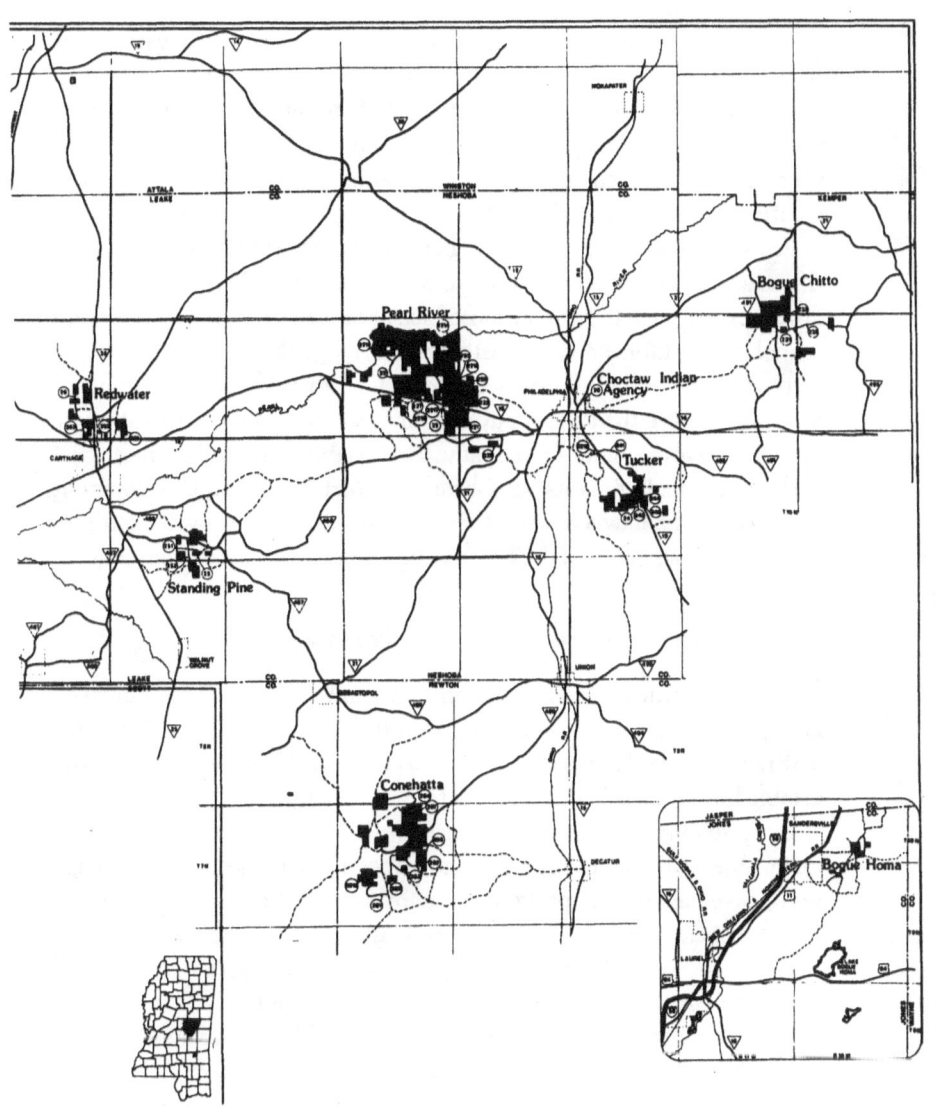

Mississippi Choctaw Indian Communities in 1984.

Mississippi Choctaw in December 1944. Then, in 1945, the Mississippi Band of Choctaw Indians reformed its tribal council and adopted a constitution and bylaws.

The federal government's early attempts at economic development focused on helping the Choctaw to switch from sharecrop farming to independent farming and to bring tribal members into the various Choctaw communities. Between 1918 and 1944 the groundwork was thus laid in the areas of education, health, land acquisition, and the creation of a tribal government.

From the early 1950s onward, giant strides continued to be made in the areas of education, health, and housing as well as in economic development and the expansion of social and human services. A high school was established at Pearl River in 1963; the Choctaw Housing Authority was established in 1965; and more than 400 homes were built, with more than 200 renovated and repaired on the reservation by the Chata Development Company. The establishment of an industrial park, with such tenants as Chata Enterprise, Chata Development Company, Choctaw Greetings Enterprise, and Choctaw Electronics Enterprise, has improved Choctaw life and economic development.

Federal Policy and Choctaw Economic Progress

Reforms advocated in the Indian Reorganization Act of 1934 allowed for a period of growth for the American Indian nationally between 1933 and 1945. for the Choctaw, it was a period of land consolidation and the establishment of tribal government.

Because of changing federal philosophies, however, by 1946 the BIA's main objective was to organize the tribes so that they could manage their own affairs, adapting their native institutions and culture to modern society, a policy called "termination." By 1950 Indian schools, clinics, and hospitals as well as tribal governments were being viewed as unnecessary. It was felt that the BIA should be abolished and federal supervision and control over the Indian should be terminated.

On August 1, 1953, Congress passed the Termination Act (House Concurrent Resolution 108). The intent of the resolution was to free Indians from federal supervision, to abolish the BIA, and to allow Native Americans to become "full-fledged" American citizens. Although many Indians, including the Choctaw, liked the idea of self-rule, they did not welcome the termination of the Indian tribes as a legal entity.

President John Kennedy's administration placed less emphasis on termination and in the early 1960s concluded that the federal policy toward the Native American was best fostered by "development rather than termination." During the 1960s, therefore, Congress passed different programs to further the economic and social development of the Indian. The Area Development Act of 1961 and its successor, the Economic Development Administration Act of 1965, made it possible for Indian reservations to receive benefits. In 1962 Indians were receiving benefits from the Manpower Development and Training Act. In that same year, the BIA organized a Division of Economic Development. With the Economic Opportunity Act of 1964, Indian communities became sponsoring agencies for such programs as Head Start and Upward Bound. Termination, however, remained the official policy until the late 1960s.

In 1968 Congress passed the Indian Civil Rights Act, which was designed for the reservation Indian and in effect replaced the 1953 policy of termination. New goals established in 1968 included raising the standard of living of the Indian, providing individuals with the option of remaining on a reservation or moving to a city, and increasing the Indian's opportunity to share in the benefits of modern America.

During the 1950s, however, while termination was the official policy, the BIA had emphasized vocational training and relocation of the Mississippi Choctaw into the mainstream of American society through the General Employment Assistance Program. The Choctaw were to receive "vocational counseling and guidance, institutional training in any recognized vocation or trade, apprenticeship, and on-the-job training either locally or in other areas."[1] Eight field employment assistance offices were established to assist in vocational training and employment assistance. These were located in Chicago, Cleveland, Dallas, Denver, Los Angeles, Oakland, San Jose, and San Francisco. Many Mississippi Choctaw participated in this program.

Although the General Employment Assistance Program meant that individuals who participated had to leave the reservation, it afforded the Choctaw the opportunity to advance both vocationally and economically. While some did return to the reservation, the program did little to improve economic development on the reservation. Overall economic and social conditions for people who remained on the reservation in the 1950s and early 1960s were extremely poor.

Evidence of poverty on the reservation during this time appears in statements made by the tribal council authorizing tribal support for the Economic Opportunity Act of 1964: "At least 90% of the Mississippi Choctaw Indians live in poverty with inadequate housing, insufficient land base and annual incomes of less than $1,000 per family . . . 75% or more are unemployed, or underemployed, and the majority have a low level of education."[2] In 1961, at the American Indian Chicago Conference, Tribal Chairman Phillip Martin reported on the status and economic conditions of the Mississippi Choctaw:

> More than half, possibly two-thirds, of the total Choctaw population live off and away from the seven reservations. Inadequate acreage of tillable and productive lands on the reservations accounts for the majority of them engaging in share-cropping. . . . The income of an average family is approximately $600.00 yearly while only a few enjoy a yearly income of approximatley $2,000.00. . . . Only a few Choctaw are skilled workers. A few are heavy road equipment operators. Most Choctaws are farm laborers. The average wage for a farm-laborer is approximately $2.50 a day which is ordinarily from sun-up to sun-down or twelve hours. . . . Farming, stock raising, poultry, pulpwood and lumber industries are the only source of income.[3]

Martin also spoke of the need for industrial development, for an increase in the hiring of Choctaw in surrounding local industries, and for improvements in education, housing, and health. He spoke against the policy of termination and against racism, segregation, and favoritism.

An early economic endeavor to help demonstrate that the Choctaw could manage their own affairs and could determine their future was their purchase of a portion of the D. L. Fair Lumber Company property more than twenty miles away at Louisville, Mississippi, and the subsequent establishment of the Louisville Cabinet Company. The first tribal resolution on this matter was recorded in August of 1963.[4] The cabinet company project was supported by BIA officials at the Choctaw Agency and was intended to provide employment for Choctaw. The plant was too far from the reservation for workers to commute, however, and consequently, few Choctaw were gainfully employed there. The experiment failed.

In March 1964 the council authorized the chairman and secretary-treasurer to execute a lease of the Louisville site with Winston Industries.[5] Eight months later the council resolved to cancel the agreement and to lease the Louisville property to Spartus Corporation, makers of clockwork devices.[6] This arrangement provided a few jobs for Choctaw, but the tribe benefited mainly from cash lease returns from this investment, using much of the money to pay off the original loan. In the late 1970s Spartus failed to renew its lease and moved most of its clock manufacturing to the Far East. The tribal council is presently developing new plans for its 17.2-acre Louisville industrial site.

In December 1966 Radio Corporation of America Service Company (RCA) entered into a contract with the BIA for the establishment, management, and operation of a vocational training center on the Choctaw Indian reservation. By this contract the BIA helped the Choctaw move a step closer to entering the mainstream of American society. It would now be possible to train Choctaw on the reservation rather than send them away for training. The RCA project was to "impart vocational skills to adult Indians, upgrade their academic education, and give them and their families sufficient experiences in city life to minimize the period of adjustment into urban society."[7]

To accomplish these goals a training center with custom-designed mobile classrooms was established, and housing of good quality was also provided to attract families. The program was intended to enable Choctaw to become self-supporting and productive individuals, although most trainees found it necessary to leave the reservation after graduation.

The vocational training program, which lasted about two years, was "designed to equip the trainee with the skills and work habits necessary to secure employment in assembly line types of occupation at unskilled and semi-skilled levels."[8] It attempted to instill good work habits and to facilitate adjustment to an urban social environment. Several graduates later found work in such cities as Jackson, Mississippi, and Memphis, Tennessee. The RCA program was at least moderately successful.

The Choctaw Land Enterprise (CLE) focused on the harvesting and marketing of the tribe's forestry and agricultural resources. The overall goal was to "promote the economic development of the Mississippi Band of Choctaw Indians and its members; to provide self-employment to its members by making land available and allowing the individual to raise his social and economic standards to a point equal to his non-Indian neighbors."[9] By the early 1970s, however, interest in further expansion of CLE had declined drastically. The tribe does continue to receive income from its timber and agricultural products and also has income from oil and gas leases with various oil drilling companies.

Income generated by the annual Choctaw Fair, which began in 1949, is a major source of tribal revenue. The costs involved in producing and sponsoring the fair, however, are considerable and significantly reduce the margin of profit. The success of the fair suggests that the tribe could attract a significant number of tourists and could develop an arts and crafts industry.

Choctaw leaders identified the potential for the development of a tribal industry during the late 1960s, when the federal government adopted a policy for the improvement of housing on Indian reservations throughout the United States. The government planned to spend billions of dollars to build new houses and to repair old ones. Since almost all Choctaw lived in substandard houses, tribal leadership realized that millions of dollars could be spent on their reservation during the next decade.

Local construction companies owned by non-Indians were of course eager for contracts to build houses for the tribe, but they seldom hired Choctaw. Since unemployment was so high, tribal leaders wanted to ensure that Choctaw were employed in building their own homes. In 1969 the tribal council authorized the creation of the Chata Development Company. The Chata Development Company (Chata), a private stock company, has a Choctaw board of directors who volunteer their time to set policies. Since 1969 almost all construction on the reservation has been done by Chata. The company has also built community centers in Conehatta, Bogue Chitto, Standing Pine, Red Water, and Bogue Homa and has played an important role in the construction of many other tribal buildings. Chata was also instrumental in the development of an industrial park on the reservation. The Choctaw leaders who originally set up Chata intended for the profits to be used to improve the economy of the tribe. Rather than distributing the profits to the stockholders, the directors of Chata have therefore reinvested in projects which have created more jobs on the reservation.

Not until the 1950s and 1960s were the Choctaw allowed to begin to implement the provisions of their 1945 constitution. The BIA continued to be a powerful force in dictating Choctaw policies during a period largely dominated by government plans for termination and relocation. Despite these obstacles Choctaw officials pushed forward in developing the reservation economically, never missing an opportunity to indicate to federal authorities that they intended to preserve their tribal identity. Experience with the Louisville Cabinet Company, the RCA Program, the Choctaw Land Enterprise, and the Chata Development Company, coupled with improvements in housing and the expanded educational opportunities that have been available since the establishment of the Choctaw Central High School, have enhanced the Choctaw sense of identity as well as improved the quality of life for all Choctaw.

Richard Nixon's presidency brought a new official attitude toward Indian policy. His administration supported "self-determination" as opposed to "termination" and stated that the Indians' future should be "determined by Indian acts and Indian decisions." The idea of self-determination can probably be traced to the 1968 Indian Civil Rights Act and emerged as a result of pressures generated by national Indian activists during the 1960s. Even though self-determination became official policy in 1970, Congress did not enact the Indian Self-Determination and Education Assistance Act (Public Law 93-638) until 1975. This act enabled tribes to participate in all social welfare programs sponsored by the federal government, allowed local tribal leaders to establish priorities and goals for their tribe without federal domination, and encouraged Indians to involve themselves in the administration of federal programs.

In 1971 the BIA initiated the Indian Business Development Act to establish and encourage Indian-owned businesses. Two years later Indian tribes became eligible to participate in the Comprehensive Employment and Training Act of 1973 (CETA). This act provided funds for manpower programs and services to assist the unemployed and economically disadvantaged. The CETA program was replaced by the Job Training Partnership Act (JTPA) in 1983. CETA emphasized employment activities; JTPA stressed training activities. By 1974 the Department of Health, Education, and Welfare had replaced the Office of Economic Opportunity as the major agency developing programs for urban Indians. Also in 1974 the Housing and Community Development Act was passed, and Indian tribes, as well as other special interest groups, were allowed to apply for and receive grants. In the early 1970s the Tribal Work Experience and Training Program was established to improve work skills. The Choctaw have participated in many other training programs, including New Careers and Operation Mainstream.

The BIA has traditionally taken a paternalistic attitude toward the Choctaw and has not allowed them to make significant decisions themselves. As the policy of self-determination evolved, Choctaw leaders began to sponsor and administer many federal programs. They also began to challenge certain BIA policies. In 1974 the tribal council, led by Chairman Phillip Martin, persuaded BIA officials in Washington to replace the superintendent and other non-Indian BIA staff officials at

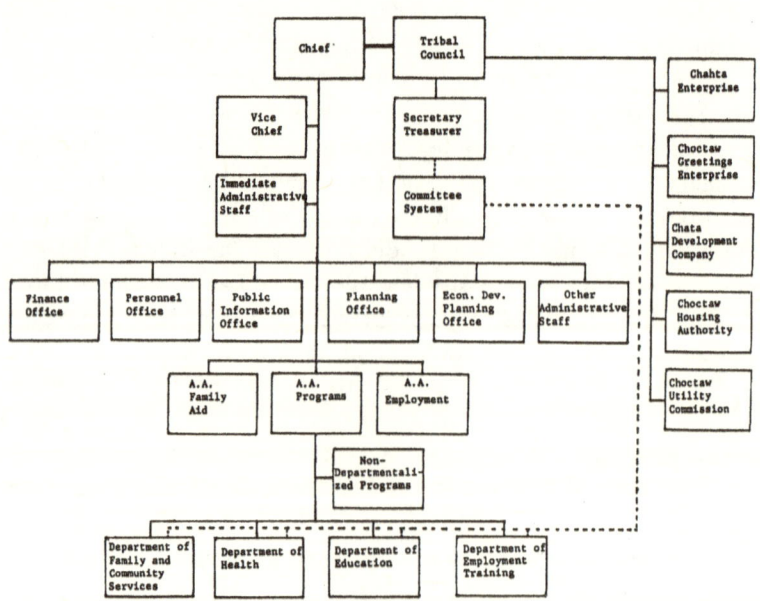

Overall organizational structure of the Mississippi Band of Choctaw Indians. *Prepared by the authors*

the Philadelphia agency with qualified Choctaw. Robert Benn of Red Water became the first Choctaw superintendent of the BIA office in Philadelphia. A graduate of Meridian High School and Mississippi College, Benn served as an officer at the agency before his appointment.

The Choctaw are continuing to assume more responsibility in determining policies on their reservation. Many of the programs formerly managed by the BIA are now operated by the Choctaw tribal government. They include the Agricultural Extension Program, Adult Education, Employment Assistance, Credit Adult Education, and housing programs. Similar changes were taking place at the Choctaw Indian Health Service, where the Choctaw Calvin Isaac of Pearl River became the service unit director in 1970. To further self-determination and to improve the social welfare of the Indian, Congress passed the Indian Health Care Improvement Act of 1976 and the Indian Child Welfare Act of 1978.

Much of the economic progress of the 1970s and 1980s can be attributed to the tribe's preparation in education and job training during the 1960s. The tribe also determined the manpower and facilities needs of prospective industrial firms and planned accordingly.

Choctaw leaders had been trying since the 1960s to persuade industrial firms to locate on the reservation. Attempts to attract Son-Nel Products of Berkeley, California, in 1960 and the McNeal Candy Company in 1969 are examples of such efforts. Frequently during the 1960s owners of industrial companies expressed uncertainty regarding the potential for success on the Choctaw reservation.

The Choctaw leaders themselves never doubted the economic and industrial potential of the reservation. The tribal council passed a resolution in October 1969 to build an industrial park at Pearl River.[10] Four years later the thirty-acre park was ready for occupancy.

In 1977 Chief Martin asked the Packard Electric Division of the General Motors Corporation, which makes electrical wiring for automobiles, to consider locating a plant on the Choctaw reservation. Six years earlier, Packard had moved most of its operation from Warren, Ohio, to Clinton, Mississippi. Like many other companies, Packard moved from the North to the South because labor costs were lower, the climate was milder, and the South was growing.

JESSE O. MCKEE AND STEVE MURRAY

By 1976 the managers at Packard's Clinton plant began to help entrepreneurs start plants in small Mississippi towns and bought the wire harnesses under a special contractual agreement. These new plants manufactured the harnesses according to directions received from Packard. Each of the plants, known as dedicated suppliers, employed about 200 persons. The first suppliers were in Lexington and Anguilla, Mississippi.

After much negotiation and careful planning, Phillip Martin and other tribal leaders convinced Packard managers that the Choctaw could produce the high-quality wire harnesses that Packard demanded. Martin, Robert Benn, and other individuals worked for many months to raise the money needed to start the company. The Economic Development Administration of the U.S. Department of Commerce provided a $346,000 grant, which was used to pay for part of the 43,000-square-foot building. The Chata Development Company gave the Wire Harness Enterprise $100,000. The rest of the money needed to start the company, more than $1 million, was borrowed from the Bank of Philadelphia. In February 1979 the first harness came off the line at the Chahta Wire Harness Enterprise.

The Chahta Wire Harness Enterprise, like the Chata Development Company, is managed by a volunteer board of directors, all of whom are members of the tribe. The company has been successful, and its parts have met GM's high stardards, offering conclusive proof that a complex industrial enterprise can be run successfully on the reservation. By 1982 the business had become so successful that the plant was expanded.

After the Chahta Wire Harness plant had been operating for a year, Martin invited American Greetings Corporation officials to visit and see the progress made since they had first visited Pearl River. At that time they had decided not to locate a plant on the reservation. The 1980 visit caused them not only to review their decision but also to change their minds.

The Choctaw Greetings Enterprise plant opened in 1981. The plant workers glue and paste ornaments on cards and make complicated folds which cannot be done economically by machine. The number of workers at the plant ranges from 150 to 300, because the greeting card business is seasonal. Unlike Chahta Wire Harness Enterprise, the Choctaw Greetings Enterprise is owned by its parent company, the American Greetings Corporation, which is responsible for all operational decisions. The Mississippi Choctaw benefit through employment and wages.

The Choctaw Greetings Enterprise's plant building in Pearl River was financed by a $4 million industrial revenue bond issue. The bonds were actually issued by the city of Philadelphia, Mississippi, since Indian tribes cannot issue their own bonds. The Choctaw Greetings Enterprise project was the first in the United States to use revenue bonds to finance a new industrial facility on an Indian reservation.

In 1985 the Choctaw attracted another industry to the reservation. A joint agreement was made with Oxford Investment Company of Chicago to manufacture automobile radio speakers. This latest economic venture, known as the Choctaw Electronics Enterprise, is located in the tribal industrial park at Pearl River and employs about sixty persons.

The Choctaw have been one of the most successful American Indian tribes in attracting and developing industry to their reservation. Their success and progress can be attributed in part to their leadership and in part to their bold spirit.

Economic Progress and Socioeconomic Development

One of the most dynamic measures of Choctaw economic success can be seen in the growing reservation population. The Mississippi Choctaw population has grown steadily since 1950, when it numbered about 2,000 persons. Between 1960 and 1970 the population increased from 2,594 to 3,016, and in 1982 the total population numbered 4,504, of whom 4,398 were Choctaw.[11] In 1980 the U.S. Bureau of the Census reported that a total of 6,131 Indians resided in the entire state of Mississippi. Approximately 70 percent of the state's Indian population lives in east central Mississippi on or near the Choctaw reservation. The Choctaw population has continued to grow during the past thirty years despite normal emigration and federal attempts at relocation.

The largest and most heavily populated reservation community is

Pearl River, followed by Bogue Chitto, Conehatta, Red Water, Tucker, Standing Pine, and Bogue Homa. Although it is not yet officially recognized as a reservation community, Crystal Ridge has a small but growing population.

In 1982 more than 60 percent of the Choctaw were under twenty-five years of age, a high percentage in comparison to the nearly 40 percent of U.S. population that is under twenty-five years of age. On the other hand only 3.3 percent of Choctaw are sixty-five years of age or older, while the U.S. average is about 11 percent. The small percentage of elderly Choctaw no doubt reflects the effects of earlier emigration as well as the comparatively low Choctaw life expectancy.

According to a survey completed in 1983, the Choctaw labor force then totaled 1,462, with 831 Choctaw employed on the reservation.[12] More than 300 Choctaw hold full-time jobs off the reservation with such companies as U.S. Electrical Motors, Wells Lamont Glove Corporation, Garan Incorporated, Molpus Lumber Company, and Weyerhaeuser Company.[13]

The largest employer on the reservation is the tribal government, which has 337 Indian employees, followed by the Bureau of Indian Affairs, with 168, Chahta Wire Harness, 161, Choctaw Greetings, 134, and Chata Development, with 31.[14] In addition, 306 non-Indians are employed on the reservation.

There has been a drastic shift in the type of work that Choctaw do. Twenty years ago more than 50 percent of the Choctaw were engaged in agricultural employment; today this figure is below 5 percent.[15] Many Choctaw today are factory workers and laborers. Sixteen percent hold professional, technical, or administrative jobs. More Choctaw are needed in key skilled and semiskilled positions, however.

The educational level of a population is critical to economic development and industrial growth. As early as 1950 only a few Choctaw had completed more than several years of schooling. By 1969 fewer than 5 percent had a high school diploma. Fewer than 20 percent had completed more than eight years of school, and fewer than 50 percent had completed more than three years of school. According to a survey taken in 1974, the median school year completed for all Choctaw was the eighth grade.[16]

Economic Development since 1945

Today the situation has improved, particularly among the younger Choctaw: 486 have graduated from high school at Pearl River, and 233 adult members of the tribe have earned high school diplomas through the Adult Education Program.[17] As of 1983 approximately 20 percent of the tribe had high school diplomas, and only 20 percent had no formal schooling.[18] Despite these favorable trends, the high school dropout rate is estimated to be about 50 percent.[19] At least eighty Choctaw have graduated from college and the tribe assists about seventy full-time and seventy-five part-time college students with college-related expenses each year.[20]

The growth in education has been accompanied by growth in income. The average household income was $1,214 in 1962 and $3,456 in 1968. By 1982 it had risen to $9,680.25.[21] Despite this improved average, nearly 24 percent of the households in 1982 earned less than $3,000 a year, and slightly more than half were below $8,000, with unemployment averaging about 22 percent.[22]

The increases in income reflect more than just an inflationary rise. The Choctaw are closing the gap with their non-Indian Mississippi counterparts. In 1970, for example, the family median income was $3,120 for Choctaw, as compared with $6,068 for the state of Mississippi and $9,590 for the nation.[23] Choctaw median income thus was about half that of the state and a third of that of the nation. By 1980 family median income for Choctaw had increased to $8,676, while the state average in 1979 was $14,603 and the national average was $19,908.[24] Choctaw median income was 59 percent of that of the state and 43 percent of that of the nation.[25]

Continual monitoring of key statistical measures will be helpful to the Choctaw in setting and attaining future goals. Certain federal programs are vital to the continuing improvements in education, health, housing, and employment. The Choctaw are making great strides, however, in taking full advantage of self-determination and in expanding their economic base. Since many young Choctaw are expressing a desire to stay on the reservation, there will be a need for more employment opportunities. Chief Martin stated in an inaugural address that one of the top priorities of his administration is job creation. If tribal officials continue to plan for economic contingencies, and if individual Choctaw continue to prepare for and work toward a progressive future, then the reservation will have the greatest possible chances for prosperity.

Notes

1. U.S. Department of Interior, Bureau of Indian Affairs, Choctaw Agency, "The Mississippi Band of Choctaw Indians," mimeographed (Philadelphia: Choctaw Agency, n.d. [1972?]), 7.
2. Choctaw Council Resolution (Cho-14-65).
3. Taken from Tribal Chairman Phillip Martin's address in Bob Ferguson, *A Choctaw Chronology*, (Nashville: Tennessee Archaeological Society, 1962), 20–21.
4. Choctaw Council Resolution (Cho-1-64).
5. Choctaw Council Resolution (Cho-16-64).
6. Choctaw Council Resolution (Cho-15-65).
7. RCA Service Company, "Training Program for Choctaw Indians" (Camden, N.J.: RCA Service Company, n.d. [1967?]), 1.
8. Ibid.
9. Choctaw Council Resolution (Cho-25-66).
10. Choctaw Council Resolution (Cho-14-70).
11. Wilbur Smith and Associates, *Comprehensive Plan, Mississippi Band of Choctaw Indians* (Columbia, S.C., 1974), 10; Mississippi Band of Choctaw Indians, "Demographic Survey" (Philadelphia, Miss., 1982), 2.
12. Steve Murray, "Analysis of the Labor Market on the Mississippi Choctaw Indian Reservation" (Mississippi State: Mississippi State University, 1983), 3, 17.
13. Ibid., 6.
14. Ibid., 26.
15. Ibid., 17; Mississippi Band of Choctaw Indians, "Demographic Survey," 13.
16. Barbara G. Spencer, John H. Peterson, Jr., and Choong S. Kim, *Choctaw Manpower and Demographic Sruvey, 1974* (Philadelphia, Miss.: Mississippi Band of Choctaw Indians, 1975).
17. Mississippi Band of Choctaw Indians, *Chahta Hapia Hoke: We Are Choctaw* (Philadelphia, Miss., 1981), 27.
18. Mississippi Band of Choctaw Indians, "Demographic Survey," 17.
19. Murray, "Analysis of the Labor Market on the Mississippi Choctaw Indian Reservation," 7.
20. Mississippi Band of Choctaw Indians, *Chahta Hapia Hoke*, 28–29.
21. Murray, "Analysis of the Labor Market on the Mississippi Choctaw Indian Reservation," 16; Mississippi Band of Choctaw Indians, "Demographic Survey," 16.
22. Ibid., 6; Murray, "Analysis of the Labor Market on the Mississippi Choctaw Indian Reservation," 20.
23. Smith and Associates, *Comprehensive Plan*, 23.
24. Murray, "Analysis of the Labor Market on the Mississippi Choctaw Indian Reservation," 18.
25. Ibid.

Selected Bibliography

Publications and Documents
of the Mississippi Band of Choctaw Indians

A Choctaw Anthology. Philadelphia: Choctaw Heritage Press, 1983.
Chahta Hapia Hoke: We Are Choctaw. Philadelphia: Miss., 1981.
Choctaw Industrial Park. Philadelphia, Miss., 1982.
"Choctaw Manpower and Demographic Survey, 1974." Philadelphia, Miss., 1975.
Choctaw Tribal Council Resolutions. 1965–70. Philadelphia, Miss.
Constitution and By-laws of the Mississippi Band of Choctaw Indians. Ratified April 20, 1945. Washington, D.C.: Government Printing Office, 1946.
"Demographic Survey." Philadelphia, Miss., 1982.
"Overall Economic Development Program, 1978–1982." Philadelphia, Miss., 1977.

Government
Documents

American State Papers: Indian Affairs. 2 vols. Washington, D.C.: Gales and Seaton, 1832–34.
American State Papers: Public Lands. 8 vols. Washington, D.C.: Gales and Seaton, 1832–61.
Bell, John. *Report on Land Claims, etc., under the Fourteenth Article of the Choctaw Treaty*. 24th Cong., 1st sess., May 11, 1836. H. Rept. 663.
Claiborne, J. F. H. *Memorial praying that the law of 1842, creating the Choctaw Commission, be repealed; and that provision be made to satisfy the just claims of the Choctaw Indians, and for their removal from the State of Mississippi*. 28th Cong., 1st sess., February 19, 1844. H. Doc. 137.
Commissioner of Indian Affairs. *Report*. 25th Cong., 3d sess., November 25, 1838. S. Doc. 1.
———. *Report*. 26th Cong., 1st sess., November 25, 1839. S. Doc. 1.
———. *Report*. 29th Cong., 1st Sess., November 30, 1845. S. Exec. Doc. 1.
———. *Report*. 30th Cong., 1st sess., November 30, 1847. S. Exec. Doc. 1.
———. *Report*. 30th Cong., 2d sess., November 30, 1848. S. Exec. Doc. 1.
———. *Report*. 31st Cong., 1st sess., November 30, 1849. S. Exec. Doc. 1.
———. *Report*. 34th Cong., 2d sess., November 22, 1856. S. Exec. Doc. 1.
———. *Report*. Washington, D.C.: Government Printing Office, 1870.
———. *Report*. 55th Cong., 3d sess., September 26, 1898. H. Doc. 5.
———. *Report*. 58th Cong., 2d sess., October 15, 1903. H. Doc. 5.
———. *Report for 1917*. Washington, D.C.: Government Printing Office, 1918.
Commission to the Five Civilized Tribes [Dawes Commission].
Five Civilized Tribes in Oklahoma. 62d Cong., 3d sess., S. Doc. 1139.
———. *Laws, Decisions, and Regulations Affecting the Work of the Commissioner to the Five Civilized Tribes, 1893–1906*. Washington, D.C.: Government Printing Office, 1906.

Selected Bibliography

———. Records. Oklahoma Historical Society, Oklahoma City.
———. Records Relating to the Mississippi Choctaws. Federal Records Center, Fort Worth, Tex.
———. *Report as to Identification of Mississippi Choctaws.* 56th Cong., 1st sess., H. Doc. 5.
———. *Report for 1904.* 58th Cong., 3d sess., H. Doc. 5.
———. *Report for 1907.* 60th Cong., 1st sess., H. Doc. 5.
———. *Report for 1908.* 60th Cong., 2d sess., H. Doc. 1046.
———. *Report Relative to the Mississippi Choctaws.* 55th Cong., 2d sess., February 3, 1898. H. Doc. 274.
———. *Report to the Secretary of the Interior for the Year Ended June 30, 1905.* Washington, D.C.: Government Printing Office, 1905.
———. *Report upon the Question Whether the Mississippi Choctaw under Their Treaties Are Not Entitled to All the Rights of Choctaw Citizenship, Except an Interest in the Choctaw Annuities.* 56th Cong., 1st sess., March 10, 1899. H. Doc. 5.
Congressional Record, 1907–16.
Federal Register.
Ingram, Mary Garland Barton. "Malmaison, Home of Greenwood Leflore." Indian Archives, Oklahoma Historical Society, Oklahoma City.
Memorial of the Choctaw Indians of the State of Mississippi to the Congress of the United States. 24th Cong., 1st sess., February 1, 1836. H. Doc. 119.
Mississippi. Clay County. Land Record Books. Chancery Clerk's Office, West Point, Miss. [Sectional Indexes, Deed Record Books, Duplicate of Original Field Notes Section, Township and Range, Field Notes, Land Tract Book 1]
———. Department of Archives and History. Territorial Governor's Records. Record Group 2. Jackson, Miss.
———. Lowndes County. Chancery Court. Cause No. 135. *Estate of Tisha Homa, Otherwise Called Captain Red Pepper.* 1836.
———. Oktibbeha County. Land Record Books. Chancery Clerk's Office, County Courthouse, Starkville, Miss. [Sectional Indexes, Deed Record Books, Duplicate of Original Field Notes Section, Township and Range, Field Notes]
———. *The Revised Code of the Statute Laws of the State of Mississippi.* Jackson: E. Barksdale, 1857.
Office of Indian Affairs. Records. Choctaw Agency Emigration. Microcopy M-234, rolls 185–87. Record Group 75. National Archives, Washington, D.C.
———. Letters Sent. Record Group 75. National Archives, Washington, D.C.
Reeves, John T. *Additional Land and Indian Schools in Mississippi.* 64th Cong., 2d sess., December 4, 1916. H. Doc. 1464.
Secretary of War. Letters Sent to the President. Record Group 107. National Archives, Washington, D.C.
———. *Report Communicating (in Compliance with a Resolution of the Senate) Information in Relation to the Contracts Made for Removal and Subsistence of the Choctaw Indians.* 28th Cong., 2d sess., February 7, 1845. S. Doc. 86.

Selected Bibliography

U.S. Congress. *Register of Debates.* 21st Cong., 1st sess., February 24, 1830, and 2d sess., April 6, 1830.

———. House of Representatives. *Mississippi Choctaws.* 54th Cong., 2d sess. March 3, 1897. H. Rpt. 3080.

———. Committee on Indian Affairs. *Hearings before the Subcommittee . . . on the Subject of Enrollment in the Five Civilized Tribes.* Washington, D.C.: Government Printing Office, 1915.

———. Committee on Investigation of the Indian Service. *Hearings.* Vol. 2: *Condition of the Mississippi Choctaws.* Washington, D.C.: Government Printing Office, 1917.

———. *Memorial of the Choctaw Nation.* 42d Cong., 3d sess., February 13, 1873. H. Misc. Doc. 94.

———. Senate. *Journal of Proceedings at the Treaty of Dancing Rabbit Creek.* 23d Cong., 1st sess., September 15–28, 1830. S. Doc. 512.

———. *Letter from the Secretary of War, in Relation to the Adjustment of Claims Arising under the Fourteenth and Nineteenth Articles of the Treaty of Dancing Rabbit Creek with the Choctaw Indians.* 27th Cong., 2d sess., March 16, 1842. S. Doc. 188.

———. *Letter from the Secretary of War, Relative to the Contracts for the Emigration of the Choctaw Indians.* 28th Cong., 2d sess., January 21, 1845. H. Doc. 107.

———. *Message from the President of the United States in Compliance with a Resolution of the Senate of the Thirteenth October, 1837, in Relation to the Adjustment of Claims to Reservations under the Fourteenth Article of the Treaty of 1830, with the Choctaw Indians.* 25th Cong., 2d sess., December 19, 1837. S. Doc. 25.

Message from the President . . . Relative to . . . the Choctaw Treaty. 29th Cong., 1st. sess. April 25, 1846. H. Exec. Doc. 189.

———. *Message from the President of the United States Transmitting the Correspondence in Relation to the Proceedings and Conduct of the Choctaw Commission, under the Treaty of Dancing Rabbit Creek.* 28th Cong., 1st sess., January 30, 1844. S. Doc. 168.

———. *Petition of John D. LeFlore and James C. Harris, Executors of the Last Will and Testament of Greenwood LeFlore.* 43rd Cong., 1st sess., April 29, 1874. S. Rept. 314.

U.S. Court of Claims. *Estate of Charles F. Winston and Others v. Jack Amos and Others, Known as the "Mississippi Choctaw."* 51 U.S. Court of Claims, No. 29821, 288 (1916).

U.S. Statutes. Vol. 5. Boston: Little, Brown, 1856.

U.S. Supreme Court. *United States v. John.* 98 Supreme Court 2541 (1978).

U.S. War Department. *The War of the Rebellion: A Compilation of the Official Record of the Union and Confederate Armies.* 70 vols. Washington, D.C.: Government Printing Office, 1880–1901.

Other Sources

Abernethey, Thomas P. *The Formative Period in Alabama, 1815–1828.* N.p., 1922.

Selected Bibliography

Amann, William F., *Personnel of the Civil War.* Vol. 1: *The Confederate Armies.* New York: Yoseloff, 1961.
Baird, W. David. *Peter Pitchlynn: Chief of the Choctaws.* Norman: University of Oklahoma Press, 1972.
Bartram, William. *Travels.* Edited by Mark Van Doren. New York: Dover, 1955.
Bassett, John Spencer, *Correspondence of Andrew Jackson.* 7 vols. Washington, D.C.: Carnegie Institution, 1926–35.
Beckett, Charles M. "Choctaw Indians in Mississippi since 1830." Master's thesis, Oklahoma Agricultural and Mechanical College, 1949.
Bernard, Mother Mary. *The Story of the Sisters of Mercy in Mississippi.* New York: Kennedy and Sons, 1931.
Bounds, Thelma V. *Children of Nanih Waiya.* San Antonio: Naylor, 1964.
Brandon, William. *The American Heritage Book of Indians.* New York: American Heritage, 1961.
Brown, A. J. *History of Newton County, Mississippi, from 1834 to 1894.* Jackson: Clarion-Ledger, 1894.
Buhite, Russell D. *Patrick J. Hurley and American Foreign Policy.* Ithaca: Cornell University Press, 1973.
Burt, Jesse, and Ferguson, Robert B. *Indians of the Southeast: Then and Now.* Nashville: Abingdon Press, 1973.
Bushnell, David I., Jr. *The Choctaw of Bayou Lacomb, St. Tamany Parish, Louisiana.* Smithsonian Institution, Bureau of American Ethnology, Bulletin 48. Washington, D.C.: Government Printing Office, 1909.
Byington, Cyrus. *A Dictionary of the Choctaw Language.* Edited by J. R. Swanton and H. S. Halbert. Smithsonian Institution, Bureau of American Ethnology, Bulletin 46. Washington, D.C.: Government Printing Office, 1915.
Choctaw Nation. *Acts and Resolutions of the General Council . . . Passed at Its Regular Session, October, 1897.* N.p.: Elevator Job Office, 1897.
―――. *Memorandum of Particulars in Which the Choctaw Nation and Individuals Are Entitled to Relief and Compensation in Case They Are Not Paid the Net Proceeds of Their Lands Ceded by the Treaty of September 27, 1830.* Washington, D.C.: Gideon, 1856.
Claiborne, J. F. H. *Mississippi as a Province, Territory, and State.* Vol. 1. Jackson: Power and Barksdale, 1880.
Cobb, Joseph B. *Mississippi Scenes; or, Sketches of Southern and Western Life and Adventure, Humorous, Satirical, and Descriptive, Including the Legend of Black Creek.* Philadelphia: A. Hart, 1851.
Coker, William S. "Pat Harrison's Efforts to Reopen the Choctaw Citizenship Rolls." *Southern Quarterly* 3 (October 1964): 36–60.
Cotterill, Robert. *The Southern Indians.* Norman: University of Oklahoma Press, 1954.
Crawford, James M. *The Mobilian Trade Language.* Knoxville: University of Tennessee Press, 1978.
Cushman, Horatio B. *History of the Choctaw, Chickasaw, and Natchez Indians.* 1899. Reprint. New York: Russell and Russell, 1972.
Davis, Christopher. *North American Indian.* London: Hamlyn, 1972.

Selected Bibliography

Davis, Edward. "The Mississippi Choctaws." *Chronicles of Oklahoma* 10 (June 1932): 257–66.
Debo, Angie. *And Still the Waters Run: The Betrayal of the Five Civilized Tribes.* Princeton: Princeton University Press Paperbacks, 1972.
―――. *The Five Civilized Tribes of Oklahoma: Report on Social and Economic Conditions.* Philadelphia: Lyon and Armor for the Indian Rights Association, 1951.
―――. *The Rise and Fall of the Choctaw Republic.* 2d ed. Norman: University of Oklahoma Press, 1961.
DeClercq, Victor C. *The Scheut Fathers in the U.S.A.* Arlington, Va.: Missionhurst, 1978.
Denevan, William M. *The Native Population of the Americas in 1492.* Madison: University of Wisconsin Press, 1976.
Densmore, Frances. *Choctaw Music.* New York: Da Capo Press, 1972.
DeRosier, Arthur H., Jr. *The Removal of the Choctaw Indians.* Knoxville: University of Tennessee Press, 1970.
Deupree, Mrs. N. D. "Greenwood Leflore." *Publications of the Mississippi Historical Society* 7 (1903): 141–52.
Durant, A. R., comp. *Constitutions and Laws of the Choctaw Nation.* Dallas: John F. Worley, 1894.
Farr, Eugene I. "Religious Assimilation: A Case Study of the Adoption of Christianity by the Choctaw Indians of Mississippi." Th.D. diss., New Orleans Baptist Theological Seminary, 1948.
―――. "A History of Baptist Missions Among the Choctaw Indians of the Bogue Homa Reservation." Master's thesis, New Orleans Baptist Bible Institute, 1942.
Ferguson, Bob. *A Choctaw Chronology.* Nashville: Tennessee Archaeological Society, 1962.
Fleming, Maureen. *Together in His Name.* New York: Sadlier, 1979.
Foreman, Grant. *Indian Removal: The Emigration of the Five Civilized Tribes of Indians.* New ed. Norman: University of Oklahoma Press, 1953.
Fritz, Henry E. *The Movement for Indian Assimilation.* Philadelphia: University of Pennsylvania Press, 1963.
Gerow, Reverend Richard. *Catholicity in Mississippi.* Marrero, La.: Hope Haven Press, 1939.
Gibson, Arrell M. *The Chickasaws.* Norman: University of Oklahoma Press, 1971.
―――. "The Indians of Mississippi." In *A History of Mississippi,* edited by Richard Aubrey McLemore. 2 vols. Hattiesburg: University and College Press of Mississippi, 1973.
Godden, Geoffrey. *Encyclopaedia of British Pottery and Porcelain Marks.* New York: Bonanza, 1964.
Guilds, John C. Introduction. In *Stories and Tales,* edited by John C. Guilds. Columbia: University of South Carolina Press, 1974.
Hafen, Leroy, R. *Western America.* Englewood Cliffs, N.J.: Prentice-Hall, 1970.
Hagan, William T. "Private Property: The Indian's Door to Civilization." *Ethnohistory* 3 (Spring 1956): 126–37.

Selected Bibliography

Halbert, H.S. "Indian Schools." In *Biennial Report of the State Superintendent of Public Education to the Legislature of Mississippi for Scholastic Years 1895–96 and 1896–97*. Jackson: Clarion-Ledger, 1898.
———. "Indian Schools in Mississippi." In *Biennial Report of the State Superintendent of Public Education to the Legislature of Mississippi for Scholastic Years 1891–92 and 1892–93*. Jackson: Clarion-Ledger, 1894.
———. "The Indians in Mississippi and Their Schools." In *Biennial Report of the State Superintendent of Public Education to the Legislature of Mississippi for Scholastic Years 1893–94 and 1894–95*. Jackson: Clarion-Ledger, 1895.
———. "The Last Indian Council on the Noxubee River." *Publications of the Mississippi Historical Society* 4 (1901):271–81.
———. "The Mississippi Choctaws." In *Biennial Report of the State Superintendent of Public Education to the Legislature of Mississippi, for Scholastic Years 1897–98 and 1898–99*. Jacksonville, Fla.: Vance, 1900.
———. "Origin of Mashulaville." *Publications of the Mississippi Historical Society* 7 (1903):389–98.
Harmon, George Dewey. *Sixty Years of Indian Affairs: Political, Economic, and Diplomatic, 1789–1850*. Chapel Hill: University of North Carolina Press, 1941.
Harris, Phil. "Malmaison—The Mansion of Leflore." *Arkansas Intelligencer*, December 22, 1845.
Hennesey, James, S.J. *American Catholics: A History of the Roman Catholic Community in the United States*. Oxford: Oxford University Press, 1981.
Holmes, William F. *The White Chief: James Kimble Vardaman*. Baton Rouge: Louisiana State University Press, 1970.
Howell, Joseph W. Report Relating to the Enrollment of Citizens and Freedmen of the Five Civilized Tribes, to the Secretary of the Interior, March 3, 1909. Choctaw Removal Records. Record Group 75. National Archives, Washington, D.C.
Hudson, Charles. *The Southeastern Indians*. Knoxville: University of Tennessee Press, 1976.
Hughes, Philip. *A Popular History of the Catholic Church*. New York: Doubleday, 1947.
Hume, Ivor Noel. *A Guide to Artifacts of Colonial America*. New York: Knopf, 1976.
Hurley, Patrick J. Papers. Box 12, file 9. Western History Collections. University of Oklahoma Library, Norman.
Jedin, Hubert. *History of the Church: The Church in the Industrial Age*. New York: Crossroad, 1981.
Jennings, Jessie D. "Chickasaw and Earlier Indian Cultures of Northeast Mississippi." *Journal of Mississippi History* 3, no. 3 (1941): 155–226.
Jones, Dorothy V. *License for Empire: Colonialism by Treaty in Early America*. Chicago: University of Chicago Press, 1982.
Kappler, Charles J., comp. and ed. *Indian Affairs: Laws and Treaties*. 5 vols. Washington, D.C.: Government Printing Office, 1904–29.
Ketcham, William H. *Kiahlik Iksa Nan-Aiyimmika I Katikisma*. Washington, D.C.: Bureau of Catholic Missions, 1916.

Selected Bibliography

Kidwell, Clara Sue, and Roberts, Charles. *The Choctaws: A Critical Bibliography.* Bloomington: Indiana University Press for the Newberry Library, 1980.
Langley, Mrs. Lee J. "Malmaison: Palace in a Wilderness, Home of General Leflore." *Chronicles of Oklahoma* 5, no. 4 (December 1927): 371–80.
Latner, Richard B. *The Presidency of Andrew Jackson: White House Politics, 1829–1837.* Athens: University of Georgia Press, 1979.
Lickteig, Franz-Bernard. "The Choctaw Indian Apostolate." *Sword* 19, no. 1 (February 1969):31–39.
———. "The Choctaw Indian Apostolate, Part II." *Sword* 19, no. 2 (June 1969):63–78.
———."The Choctaw Indian Apostolate, Part III." *Sword* 19, no. 3 (October 1969):41–58.
Lindquist, G. E. *The Red Man in the United States: An Intimate Study of the Social, Economic, and Religious Life of the American Indian.* New York: Doran, 1923.
Lipscomb, W. L. *A History of Columbus, Mississippi.* Birmingham, Ala.: Press of Dispatch Printing, 1909.
Lohbeck, Don. *Patrick J. Hurley.* Chicago: Regnery, 1956.
Lynch, Donald Reverend. "The Choctaws," *Missionary Servant Magazine,* September 1950. 12–18.
———. "Hali-to Means Hello," *Missionary Servant Magazine,* December 1952. 20–24.
McIntosh, James T., ed. *The Papers of Jefferson Davis.* Vol. 2: *June 1841–July 1846.* Baton Rouge, Louisiana State University Press, 1974.
McKee, Jesse O., and Schlenker, Jon A. *The Choctaws: Cultural Evolution of a Native American Tribe.* Jackson: University Press of Mississippi, 1980.
McLemore, Richard Aubrey, ed. *A History of Mississippi.* 2 vols. Hattiesburg: University and College Press of Mississippi, 1973.
Mainfort, Robert C., Jr. *Indian Social Dynamics in the Period of European Contact: Fletcher Site Cemetery, Bay County, Michigan.* Publications of the Museum, Michigan State University Anthropological Services 1, no. 4 (1979).
"Malmaison and Its Memories." Choctaw Agency, Bureau of Indian Affairs, Philadelphia, Miss.
Marshall, Richard A. "An Example of Chickachae Combed Pottery." *Mississippi Archaeology* 13, no. 1 (1978). 23–24.
Memorial of the Choctaw and Chickasaw Nations Relative to the Rights of the Mississippi Choctaws. Washington, D.C.: N.p., 1913.
Miller, George L. "Classification and Economic Scaling of Nineteenth Century Ceramics." *Historical Archaeology* 14 (1980).
Moore, N. Hudson. *The Old China Book.* New York: Tudor Publishing Company, 1937.
Moore, Parker L. *"Pat" Hurley: The Story of an American.* New York: Brewer, Warren and Putnam, 1932.
Moreland, George. "Life on the Indian Reservation." *Commercial Appeal,* April 29, 1934.
Murray, Steve. "Analysis of the Labor Market on the Mississippi Choctaw Indian Reservation." Mississippi State: Mississippi State University, 1983.

Selected Bibliography

Olmsted, Frederick Law. *A Journey in the Back Country.* 1860. Reprint. New York: Schocken Books, 1970.

Osoinach, H. Kirkland. "The Dynamics of Mississippi Choctaw Society: An Exploratory Formulation." Master's thesis, University of Chicago, Department of Anthropology, 1960.

Otis, D. S. *The Dawes Act and the Allotment of Indian Lands.* Edited by Francis Paul Prucha. Norman: University of Oklahoma Press, 1973.

Peterson, John H., Jr. "Louisiana Choctaw Life at the End of the Eighteenth Century." In *Four Centuries of Southern Indians,* edited by Charles Hudson. Athens: University of Georgia Press, 1975.

———. "The Mississippi Band of Choctaw Indians: Their Recent History and Current Social Relations." P:h.D. diss., University of Georgia, 1970.

———. "Three Efforts at Development among the Choctaw of Mississippi." In *Southeastern Indians since the Removal Era,* edited by Walter L. Williams. Athens: University of Georgia Press, 1979.

Penman, John T., Jr. "Archaeology and Choctaw Removal." In *Southeastern Natives and Their Pasts: A Collection of Papers Honoring Dr. Robert E. Bell.* Oklahoma Archaeological Survey Studies in Oklahoma's Past. Norman, Okla.: Noll, 1983.

———. "Historic Choctaw Towns of the Southern Division." *Journal of Mississippi History* 40, no. 2 (1978):132–41.

Pickett, A. J. *History of Alabama and Incidentally of Georgia and Mississippi.* 2 vols. 1851. Reprint. Sheffield, Ala.: R. C. Randolph, 1896.

Priest, Loring Benson. *Uncle Sam's Stepchildren: The Reformation of United States Indian Policy, 1865–1887.* New Brunswick, N.J.: Rutgers University Press, 1942.

Prucha, Francis Paul. *American Indian Policy in the Formative Years: The Indian Trade and Intercourse Acts, 1790–1834.* Cambridge, Mass.: Harvard University Press, 1962.

———. "Andrew Jackson's Indian Policy: A Reassessment." *Journal of American History* 56 (December 1969):527–39.

———, ed. *Cherokee Removal: The "William Penn" Essays and Other Writings.* Knoxville: University of Tennessee Press, 1981.

Quimby, George Irvin. *Indian Culture and European Trade Goods.* Madison: University of Wisconsin Press, 1966.

Ray, Florence Rebecca. *Chieftain Greenwood LeFlore and the Choctaw Indians of the Mississippi Valley: Last Chief of Choctaws East of Mississippi River.* 2d ed. Memphis: C. A. Davis, 1936.

RCA Service Company. "Training Program for Choctaw Indians." Camden, N.J., 1967.

Remini, Robert V. *Andrew Jackson and the Course of American Democracy.* 3 vols. New York: Harper and Row, 1977–84.

Richardson, James D., comp. *A Compilation of the Messages and Papers of the Presidents.* 10 vols. Washington, D.C.: Government Printing Office, 1896–99.

Rights of the Mississippi Choctaw. Vertical files, Choctaw Indians. Oklahoma Historical Society, Oklahoma City.

Selected Bibliography

Riley, Franklin L., "Choctaw Land Claims." *Publications of the Mississippi Historical Society* 8 (1904):345–95.
Robertson, Dario F. "The Catholic Mission and Indian Reservation." *Social Thought* Fall 1977. 15–29.
Rogin, Michael Paul. *Fathers and Children: Andrew Jackson and the Subjugation of the American Indian.* New York: Knopf, 1975.
Rowland, Dunbar. *History of Mississippi.* Chicago: S. J. Clarke, 1925.
Royce, Charles C. *Indian Land Cessions in the United States.* Eighteenth Annual Report of the U.S. Bureau of American Ethnology, 1896–97. Washington, D.C.: Government Printing Office, 1899.
Satz, Ronald N. *American Indian Policy in the Jacksonian Era.* Lincoln: University of Nebraska Press, 1975.
———. "Thomas Hartley Crawford, 1838–45." In *The Commissioners of Indian Affairs, 1824–1977,* edited by Robert M. Kvasnicka and Herman J. Viola. Lincoln: University of Nebraska Press, 1979.
Shea, John Gilmary. *History of the Catholic Missions among the Indian Tribes.* New York: P. J. Kennedy and Sons, 1854.
Shelton, Bill. "Choctaw Traditions Blend with Modern Age." *Jackson Clarion Ledger,* August 20, 1950.
Smith, Buckingham, trans. *Narratives of the Career of Hernando de Soto.* New York: Allerton, 1922.
Smith, H. Shelton. *American Christianity—1607–1820.* New York: Scribner's, 1960.
Smith, Wilbur, and Associates. *Comprehensive Plan, Mississippi Band of Choctaw Indians.* Columbia, S.C., 1974.
Sparger, Julia K. "Young Ardmore." *Chronicles of Oklahoma* 43, no. 4 (Winter 1965–66):394–415.
Strickland, Rennard. *The Indians in Oklahoma.* Norman: University of Oklahoma Press, 1980.
Swanton, John R. *Source Material for the Social and Ceremonial Life of the Choctaw Indians.* Bureau of American Ethnology, Bulletin 103. Washington, D.C.: Government Printing Office, 1931.
Sydnor, Charles S. *Slavery in Mississippi.* Baton Rouge: Louisiana State University Press, 1966.
Thompson, Bobby, and Peterson, John H., Jr. "Mississippi Choctaw Identity: Genesis and Change." In *The New Ethnicity: Perspectives from Ethnology,* edited by John W. Bennett. St. Paul: West, 1975.
Thorpe, Francis Newton. *The Federal and State Constitutions.* 7 vols. Washington, D.C.: Government Printing Office, 1909.
Tolbert, Charles Madden. "A Sociological Study of the Choctaw Indians in Mississippi." Ph.D. diss., Louisiana State University, Department of Sociology. 1958.
Valliere, Kenneth L. "The Creek War of 1836: A Military History." *Chronicles of Oklahoma* 57 (Winter 1979–80):463–85.
Van Every, Dale. *Disinherited: The Lost Birthright of the American Indian.* New York: Avon, 1966.
Varner, John Grier, and Varner, Jeanette Johnson, eds. and trans. *The Florida of the Inca.* Austin: University of Texas Press, 1951.

Selected Bibliography

Wade, John William. "The Removal of the Mississippi Choctaws." *Publications of the Mississippi Historical Society* 8 (1904):397–426.
Ward, Rufus A., Jr. "English Earthenwares Associated with Early Nineteenth Century Choctaw Sites." *Mississippi Archaeology* 18 (1983):37–45.
Warner, Ezra J. *Generals in Gray: Lives of the Confederate Commanders.* Baton Rouge: Louisiana State University Press, 1959.
Washburn, Wilcomb E. *The Indian in America.* New York: Harper and Row, 1975.
———. *Red Man's Land—White Man's Law: A Study of the Past and Present Status of the American Indian.* New York: Scribner's, 1971.
Wells, Samuel J. "Counting Countrymen on the Tombigbee." *Southern Historian* 4 (Spring 1983):2–11.
Wharton, Vernon Lane. *The Negro in Mississippi, 1865–1890.* Chapel Hill: University of North Carolina Press, 1947.
Williams, Walter L., ed. *Southeastern Indians since the Removal Era.* Athens: University of Georgia Press, 1979.
Wilson, Eugene M. *Alabama Folk Houses.* Montgomery: Alabama Historical Commission, 1975.
York, Kenneth H. "Mobilian: The Indian *Lingua Franca* of Colonial Louisiana." In *La Salle and His Legacy: Frenchmen and Indians in the Lower Mississippi Valley,* edited by Patricia K. Galloway. Jackson: University Press of Mississippi, 1983.
Young, Mary E. "Indian Removal and Land Allotment: The Civilized Tribes and Jacksonian Justice." *American Historical Review* 64 (October 1958):31–45.
———. *Redskins, Ruffleshirts, and Rednecks: Indian Allotments in Alabama and Mississippi, 1830–1860.* Norman: University of Oklahoma Press, 1961.

Contributors

R. HALLIBURTON, JR., is the chairman of the department of history at Northeastern State University, Tahlequah, Oklahoma. He has published numerous articles on American Indians and related topics as well as several books, including *Red Over Black: Black Slavery in the Cherokee Nation*.

CLARA SUE KIDWELL is an associate professor at the University of California at Berkeley. She has taught in Native American or American Indian studies programs at the University of Minnesota and at the Haskell Indian Junior College. She is coauthor of *The Choctaws: A Critical Bibliography*.

SISTER JOHN CHRISTOPHER LANGFORD, M.S.B.T., is a member of the Missionary Servants of the Most Blessed Trinity and has spent ten years with the Mississippi Choctaw.

JESSE O. MCKEE is chair of the department of geography and area development at the University of Southern Mississippi. He is coauthor of *The Choctaws: Cultural Evolution of a Native American Tribe*, and recently edited *Ethnicity in Contemporary America: A Geographical Appraisal*.

STEVE MURRAY is a community development specialist with the Mississippi Cooperative Extension Service. He worked for the Mississippi Band of Choctaw Indians as a planner from 1971 to 1975, and has been a financial consultant with them since 1977.

CHARLES ROBERTS is a professor of Native American history and literature at California State University, Sacramento. He is the coauthor of *The Choctaws: A Critical Bibliography*.

RONALD N. SATZ is dean of the graduate school, director of research, and professor of history at the University of Wisconsin-Eau Claire. In addition to numerous articles and book reviews, his published work includes *American Indian Policy in the Jacksonian Era*.

RUFUS WARD is an attorney in West Point, Mississippi. He is on the Board of Advisors of the National Trust for Historic Preservation and

Contributors

has served as northern vice-president of the Mississippi Archaeological Association.

SAMUEL J. WELLS has served as an editorial consultant for the Mississippi Band of Choctaw Indians and has published several articles on the Mississippi Choctaw.

Index

Ames, James, mentioned, 100
An-o-ka-chub-bee, mentioned, 75
Angell, William H., Role as land office commissioner, 103–7
Annouchi, Moontubbee, memorialist, 68
Armstrong, F. W., compiles Choctaw removal census, 65
Atoka Indian Citizen, mentioned, 97

Baker, Jesse, assists Peter Folsom, 83
Barton, Roger, joins claims commission, 69, 72
Bayless, Thomas, places removed Choctaw on homesteads, 106–7
Bekkers, Father B. J.: mentioned, 84, 95–96; establishes Holy Rosary Mission, 112–15
Benn, Robert, assists Martin and others in raising funds, 132
Bethany Baptist church, mentioned, 95
Billey, Rena, receives letter regarding her removal, 101
Billy, Tom: mentioned, 96; acts as church miko, 112–15
Billy, Willy, son of Tom Billy, 113
Bishop Gunn, Bishop of Natchez, 117
Black Jack Methodist church, mentioned, 95, 108
Bogue Chitto clan, population of, 79
Bohannon, Siles, reservation of, 37
Bonaparte, Josephine, Maimaison named in honor of, 59
Bowman, agent, distributes scrip, 80
Brown, James, replaces Jesse Baker, 83
Brown, Nola Leflore, born at Malmaison, 62
Brown, Orlando, Whig Indian commissioner, 14
Bureau of Indian Affairs (BIA), economic acts and programs, 125–30
Byington, Cyrus, translates Bible and hymns into Choctaw, 81

Campbell, Anthony, U. S. Marshall, witnesses harassment of Choctaw, 9
Cass, Lewis, secretary of war, mentioned, 66
Catholic religious orders assigned to assist Mississippi Choctaw, 114–19
Cattle: mentioned, 16; introduction of into Choctaw country, 47
Cherokee Indians, mentioned, 53
Chickachae pottery, mentioned, 34, 38
Chickasaw Indians: mentioned, 46, 53; intermarriage with whites, 47
Chief Cobb, quoted, 11–12
Choctaw claims: mentioned, 13, 21, 65–68, 78, 80, 86, 97; commission on, 68–74, 76–77
Choctaw communities, mentioned, 22–23, 33, 84–85
Choctaw Council house, description of, 34
Choctaw nation: mentioned, 51, 86, 96. *See also* Oklahoma Choctaw
Choctaw nation: rolls, 21–23, 108
Chunka clan, population of, 79
Claiborne, John F. H.: quoted, 15–16; mentioned, 72; criticizes Indian commission, 75–77
Cobb, Joseph Beckham, quoted on Choctaw condition in 1851, 16–17
Cooper, Douglas H.: mentioned, 17, 79, 80; Cooper roll, 79
Cooper, Floyd, mentioned, 100
Countrymen (whites residing in Indian country), mentioned, 42, 45–46, 51, 74
Cravat, John, countryman, mentioned, 47
Cravat, Rebecca wife of Louis Le Fleur, 56
Crawford, Thomas Hartford (commissioner of Indian affairs), mentioned, 10–11, 13, 77
Creek Indians, mentioned, 46, 53
Cumby, Olmon, quoted, 22–23
Curtis act of 1898, mentioned, 21, 86, 94, 97

149

Index

Davis, Jefferson: quoted, 13, 14; describes conditions of Indians, 36
Dawes act, See General Allotment act of 1887
Dawes commission, mentioned, 86, 87, 97–99, 103, 105, 106
Dawes, Henry F., heads Dawes commission, 97
Deignan, Father Francis, pastor of Holy Rosary Mission, 1932–1944, 118
Dickerson, Mahlon, acting secretary of war, encourages Choctaw claims, 66
Donley, John, befriends Greenwood Leflore, 56
Donley, Rosa, wife of Greenwood Leflore, 56
Duchess of Orleans, mentioned, 61

Eaton, John, mentioned, 3–7
Enis, Father, pastor, Holy Rosary mission, 116

Fisher, Charles, claims attorney, mentioned, 70, 73, 75
Folsom, David: mentioned, 47, quoted, 49
Folsom, Nathaniel, father of David Folsom, 47
Folsom, Peter, mentioned, 83, 95
Folsom, Rhoda Nail, wife of David Folsom, 47, 48
Folsom, Sophia, mother of David Folsom, 48
Folsom, William W., escorts removing Choctaw, 106
French Camp, mentioned, 56
Fulton, J. S., contracted to treat sick Choctaw, 106

Garland, Thomas, 37. See also Wall, Thomas
General Allotment Act of 1887 (Dawes Act), mentioned, 20, 85
Grant, Reuben H., mentioned, 74
Graves, Ralph: named to Indian commission in 1842, 72; mentioned, 74; quarrels with Claiborne, 75
Gresset, agent, mentioned, 100
Gwin, Daniel, mentioned, 75

Gwin, Doctor, mentioned, 70
Gwin, Edward, mentioned, 75
Gwin, William M., mentioned, 75, 76

Halbert, Henry Sales: assigned as mission school teacher, 84, mentioned, 85, 96, 113
Haloon Iowah clan, population of, 79
Haney, Jim, mentioned, 100
Harkins, George W., replaces Greenwood Leflore as Choctaw chief, 58
Harris, James C.: mentioned, 59; marries Rebecca Leflore, 61
Hitchcock, E. A., authorizes removing Mississippi Choctaw in 1903, 98
Holland, J., family of, 112
Holy Rosary church, established by 1884, 95
Honey Springs church, removal camp located at, 107
Hopah-cha-nubbee, memorialist, 68
Hopahka, residence of Colonel Forester, mentioned, 75, 76
Hopewell Baptist church, 83
Hotana reservation, location of, 37
Hurley, Patrick J., attorney for Choctaw nation, 22

Indian act of 1918, 116
Indian Civil Rights act of 1968, 125
Indian Commission of 1842, 15, 72
Indian Removal Act of 1830, implementation of in Mississippi, 3–6
Isaac, Calvin, named health service director on 1970, 131
Isom, Wilson, mentioned, 100

Jack, Jim, mentioned, 113
Jackson, Andrew, Indian policy of, 3–6, 8–10, 53, 67
Jackson, Solomon, mentioned, 103
Janssens, Francis, Bishop of Natchez, mentioned, 95, 112, 113
Jasper, Martha, mentioned, 100
Joshua, Joe, mentioned, 100
Juzan, Pierre, early French countryman, 47

Index

Kendall, Gus C., mentioned, 102
Ketcham, William H., director of Catholic Indian Missions, assistance of, 115–17
Kirksey, E. B. W., letter quoted, 73. *See also* Poindexter, James

Labatche clan, population of, 79
LaFleur, Louis, mentioned, 47. *See also* Le Fleur
LaFleur, Michael, mentioned, 47
Land allotments, mentioned, 5, 7, 22, 51, 64
Land speculation, mentioned, 8, 10, 13, 15, 16, 21, 66, 68, 71, 74, 75, 77, 78–79
Lane, Franklin K., secretary of interior, mentioned, 23
Le Fleur's Bluff, mentioned, 56
Le Fleur, Louis, mentioned, 56. *See also* LaFleur
Leflore, Greenwood: mentioned, 15, 17, 47; success of, 56–63
Lewis, Hudson, mentioned, 100
Lewis, Moses, mentioned, 75
Lincecum, Grabel, testifies against William Ward, 67
Little Leader (Opie Sketona), mentioned, 68, 70, 75
Long, T. J., contracted to treat sick Choctaw, 106
Lynch, Father Donald, mentioned, 119

Macedonia Baptist church, 95
Malmaison, described, 59–63
Manypenny, George, commissioner of Indian affairs, 80
Martin, George W., actions in Mississippi as government agent, 65–71, 65
Martin, Phillip, tribal chairman, chief, mentioned, 126, 130–32
McCurtain, Green, principal Oklahoma Choctaw chief, 101
McDonald, James, articulate mixed-blood, 51
McKenna, Father J. T., pastor of Holy Rosary mission, 118
McKennon, A. S., member of 1898 commission to remove Choctaw, 97

McKenny, Thomas Loraine, secretary of Indian Affairs, 51
McKinley, John, first superintendent of Mississippi Choctaw agency, 117
McRae, John, enrolls Choctaw at Hopahka, 76, 77
Mississippi Band of Choctaw Indians: organized, 23; economic enterprises, 124; High school established in 1963, 124; reservation established in 1944, 124; Annual Choctaw fair, 128; community centers, 128; population of, 133; communities, 134; demographics, 135
Mississippi Baptist Association, mentioned, 83
Mississippi Choctaw: population of, 48, 65, 68, 77, 79, 86, 87, 96, 97, 100; schools, 84, 88; agency created in 1918, 89, 117; Baptist churches, 95; Methodist churches, 95, 108; Catholic churches, 95, 108, 112–21; communities mentioned, 96, 103, 117–19, 121
Mississippi, Indian policy of, 9, 15, 18, 84
Mixed-bloods: mentioned, 6, 7, 9, 15, 17, 56, 65, 98, 107; role of, 42–55; listed, 43, 50
Moglusha clan, population of, 79
Moshulitubbee: mentioned, 34; house of, 35
Mount Zion Baptist church, mentioned, 95

Nail, Rhoda, wife of David Folsom, 47
Natchez Trace, mentioned, 56
New Choctaw Baptist Association, formed in 1911, 87
Nitakechi, mentioned, 13
Norton, Patrick, congressman holding hearings on plight of Mississippi Choctaw, 22

Ohoyo, Aiahnichih, wife of Nathaniel Folsom, 47
Oklahoma Indian policy, 22
Oklahoma Baptist church, 83
Oklahoma Choctaw: mentioned, 18, 19; missionaries to Mississippi Choctaw, 95
Old Jefferson, mentioned, 113

Index

Olmstead, Frederick Law, mentioned, 17
Owen, Robert L., attorney soliciting Indian claims contracts, 20, 21, 98

Patterson, Carl, ordered to prepare Oklahoma homestead plats, 105
Pearl River clan, population of, 79
Peedon, Howell, mentioned, 37
Pemberton, John C. commanded Mississippi Choctaw Infantry Battalion during Civil war, 18
Phillipe, Father Edmond, Catholic missionary, 117–18
Phillips, Willie, mentioned, 113
Pitchlynn, John, early British countryman, 48
Pitchlynn, Peter, son of John Pitchlynn, 48
Poindexter, James, letter quoted, 73. *See also* Kirksey, E. B. W.
Pray, Publius R. R., Choctaw claims commissioner, 69

Queen and Crescent Railway, use of for second removal, 102–3

Red Post Oak, memorialist, 68
Reeves, John R. T., reports on condition of Choctaw schools, 88

Scott, Christopher C., mentioned, 75
Scrip certificates: issue of, 11–14, 72–73; use of to force removal, 76–80
Sells, Cato, commissioner of Indian affairs, visits Mississippi Choctaw, 23
Sharecropping, mentioned, 19, 82, 83, 124
Sharman, R. J., contracts to provide medical service, 102
Simpson, Bernard, mentioned, 113
Simpson, George, telephones Green McCurtain, 101
Simpson, Gill, mentioned, 100
Six Towns district, mentioned, 47
Six Towns clan, population of, 79
Sketona, Opie (alias Little Leader), mentioned, 75
Slaves, mentioned, 6, 15, 58, 59, 62, 82
Smith, H. Van V., role of as removal agent, 96–108

Soloman, Willie, mentioned, 100
Spencer, J. C., secretary of War, recommends use money to pay Choctaw claims, 71–72
Standley, James S., contracts to bring Mississippi Choctaw to Oklahoma, 96
Stickball, mentioned, 81, 83, 85, 103
Sukanache clan, population of, 79

Ta-wam-tucha, mentioned, 75
Talla chulak clan, population of, 79
Termination act of 1953, 124
Thomas, George, queries Smith on removal, 101
Tisha Homa, inventory of, 34–36
Tories, mentioned, 45–46
Treaty of Dancing Rabbit Creek: Article 14, effect on Choctaw, 5–11, 20, 64–66, 94; mentioned, 6, 49; Article 19, mentioned, 64
Treaty of Hopewell, mentioned, 48
Tubby, Simson: establishes Methodist church, 95; mentioned, 108
Tush ka la meta clan, population of, 79
Tyler, William, replaces Barton on claims commission, 73

United States v. John, 1978 supreme court decision affirming status of Mississippi Band of Choctaw Indians, 23

Van Buren, Martin, mentioned, 10
Venable, William, Mississippi congressman requests hearing on plight of Choctaw in 1917, 22
Verhoven, Joseph, Catholic missioniary, 117
Vroom, P. D., appointed Indian claims commissioner, 69

Wall, Thomas (alias Thomas Garland), mentioned, 37
Wallace, Jim, mentioned, 100
Ward's register: mentioned, 9, 80; inaccuracy of, 65–69
Ward, William, role of as Choctaw agent, 7–9, 65, 70
West, Benjamin, noted painter, 61

Index

Whigs, mentioned, 10–16
Whitsett, John C., mentioned, 75
Wickson, Sim, quoted, 101
William, John, mentioned, 100, 101
Williams, John Sharp, Mississippi congressman, defends Choctaw rights, 20–21
Wilson, Charles F., speculator in Choctaw land allotments, 98

Wilson, Woodrow, mentioned, 23
Winton, Charles F., attorney soliciting Indian claims contracts, 20, 21
Word, T. J., role as special agent, 75–76
Wright, Daniel W., land speculator, 70, 75

Yokatubbee reservation, location of, 38
York nuk ne clan, population of, 79
Young, Alexander F., mentioned, 75

www.ingramcontent.com/pod-product-compliance
Lightning Source LLC
Chambersburg PA
CBHW030345240426
43661CB00052B/1744